3-91

The Macmillan Pre-Vocation

Series editor
Douglas Pride

Core Skills in Numeracy

Richard Musgrove

M

Macmillan Education

Acknowledgements

The author and publishers wish to acknowledge the following sources: J. Allan Cash, pp. 37, 95 bottom; British Rail, pp. 74, 75; British Telecom, p. 85; Jim Brownbill, p. 8; HMSO Central Statistical Office, p. 32; Horizon Holidays Ltd, p. 14; Modern Furniture Co, p. 16; Motor Licensing Office, Department of Transport, pp. 8, 9; National Union of Public Employees, p. 34; Supreme Ltd, p. 22; Thompson Holidays, p. 14; TSB England and Wales, p. 20.

The publishers have made every effort to trace copyright holders, but where they have failed to do so they will be pleased to make the necessary arrangements at the first opportunity.

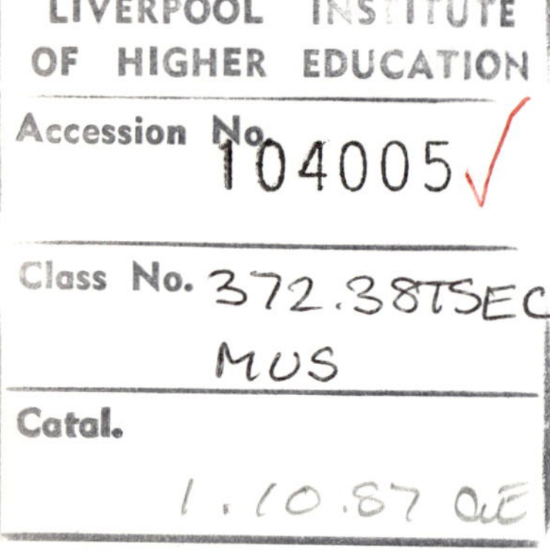
LIVERPOOL INSTITUTE OF HIGHER EDUCATION
Accession No. 104005
Class No. 372.38TSEC MUS
Catal. 1.10.87 QE

© Richard Musgrove 1986

All rights reserved. No reproduction, copy or transmission of this publication may be made without written permission.

No paragraph of this publication may be reproduced, copied or transmitted save with written permission or in accordance with the provisions of the Copyright Act 1956 (as amended).

Any person who does any unauthorised act in relation to this publication may be liable to criminal prosecution and civil claims for damages.

First published 1986
Reprinted 1987

Published by
MACMILLAN EDUCATION LTD
Houndmills, Basingstoke, Hampshire RG21 2XS
and London
Companies and representatives
throughout the world

Printed and bound in Great Britain by
Anchor Brendon Ltd, Tiptree, Essex

British Library Cataloguing in Publication Data
Musgrove, Richard
Core skills in numeracy—
(The Macmillan Pre-Vocational Series)
1. Numeracy—Problems, exercises, etc.
I. Title
513′.076 QA139
ISBN 0-333-39599-9

Contents

Introduction

This series is designed to help students meet the criteria laid down by the Joint Board for the new Certificate of Pre-Vocational Education. It aims to fulfil the three main requirements of CPVE courses:

(a) the integration of a core of basic skills with a wide-ranging choice of vocational studies;
(b) activity-based learning; and
(c) a flexibility that enables courses to be tailored to the needs of individual students.

The books in the series are arranged in two groups: one group concentrates on developing the main core competences, using different vocational settings; the other concentrates on the skills required in the vocational categories (the CPVE introductory and exploratory modules), but also provide practice in the core competences.

Each book consists of twenty assignments which develop skills in both general and specific vocational contexts. Ten of these concentrate on skills in general vocational contexts and ten on specific vocational situations (see diagram).

Main core competences

Core Skills in Communication	*Core Skills in Numeracy*	*Core Skills in Industrial, Social and Environmental Studies*	*Core Skills in Science and Technology*	*Core Skills in Information Technology*

10 Core assignments (general vocational contexts)
10 Focus assignments (specific vocational situations)
10 Information pages

Course

Vocational skills

10 Introductory assignments (general vocational contexts)
10 Exploratory assignments (specific vocational situations)
10 Information pages

Core Skills in Business and Administrative Services	*Core Skills in Information Technology and Micro-electronic Systems*	*Core Skills in Service Engineering*	*Core Skills in Manufacture*	*Core Skills in Craft-based Activities*	*Core Skills in Distribution*	*Core Skills in Services to People*

The assignments are free-standing and can be combined in different modular ways according to individual course needs. To assist selection and combination, the objectives of each assignment are given both at its head and in a grid at the beginning of each book. At the end of each book information pages give facts and advice to support the activities in the assignments.

Core Skills in Numeracy has ten core assignments which develop and practise numerical and spatial concepts through familiar everyday activities and contexts. The development and practice of these competences is also carried out in the vocational situations of the focus assignments. The ten information pages provide guidance on basic concepts and operations such as place value, percentages, area and volume, averages and use of the calculator.

The material in this volume is also suitable for a wide range of other numeracy teaching, such as in: YTS off-the-job training; National Certificate (Scotland); RSA Vocational Preparation (clerical, distribution); CGLI Foundation Courses and Certificate in Numeracy Skills; AEB Test in Basic Arithmetic; and developing BTEC courses.

CPVE grid

Assignments \ CPVE aims in Numeracy	1.1	1.2	1.3	1.4	1.5	1.6	1.7	1.8	1.9	1.10	1.11	1.12	1.13	1.14	1.15	1.16	1.17	1.18	1.19	1.20	2.1	2.2	2.3	2.4	2.5	2.6	2.7	2.8	2.9	2.10	2.11	2.12	2.13	2.14	2.15	2.16
1 On the road	■		■			■	■						■		■					■																
2 Can I afford it?	■		■			■							■		■					■																■
3 Getting to grips with credit	■	■	■			■							■		■					■																
4 Cost of living	■		■			■	■						■	■	■					■															■	
5 Tax	■		■			■	■	■					■	■						■															■	
6 Pay packet	■		■		■	■	■						■	■	■					■																
7 Room to move	■		■							■		■		■									■		■	■			■		■					
8 Air to breathe	■	■	■							■		■		■				■					■													
9 Keep the noise down	■		■							■																									■	
10 Drawn to scale	■		■						■	■										■			■	■			■					■	■	■		
11 Cooking for crowds	■		■						■		■	■								■											■					■
12 Constructive ideas	■		■			■				■				■	■					■		■	■			■										
13 Paperwork	■		■											■	■					■																
14 In the workshop	■		■			■						■	■		■				■	■	■			■												
15 Comings and goings	■		■			■									■					■																
16 On sale	■		■			■	■	■												■																■
17 Solid	■		■		■	■			■	■				■						■			■	■					■							
18 At the office	■		■			■	■							■						■																
19 On the shelf	■	■	■																	■																
20 From the cradle to the grave	■		■	■			■			■	■					■		■		■												■			■	

Core assignments

1 On the road

AIM

To develop your skills in
- using a table of figures
- making percentage-discount calculations
- doing both approximate and exact calculations using pencil and paper and using a calculator
- assessing some of the costs of running a motorcycle

Introduction

How much does it cost to get a moped or motorcycle on the road? There is the cost of the bike, but that's not all. There are also insurance, vehicle excise duty (the tax disc), and things like crash helmets to buy as well.

Insurance

Third-party, fire and theft and *comprehensive* insurance are the two basic choices.

'Third-party, fire and theft' covers any claim against you by another person. This other person is called the 'third party'. If you ride the bike into someone's car, for instance, the insurance company will pay for the car to be repaired. The insurance company will not pay for you to have your bike fixed, though. However, if your bike is damaged by fire, or stolen, you can claim compensation under this type of insurance.

Comprehensive insurance will pay for your bike to be repaired even if the damage was caused through your own fault. Because of this, comprehensive insurance costs more than third-party, fire and theft insurance.

Figure 1 is a table of insurance premiums (the cost per year) issued by one company. As you can see, the cost of insurance varies with your age and also with the bike's engine capacity.

Figure 1 Insurance premiums

Premiums
Applicable to all UK except London, Liverpool and Glasgow areas, and Northern Ireland

			Comprehensive		
Age	**16/17**	**18/19**	**20/21**	**22/24**	**25+**
Mopeds	£90	£60	£45	£30	£20
51–100 cc	£100	£80	£60	£40	£20
101–250 cc	£350	£330	£250	£150	£70
251–350 cc	£425	£390	£275	£175	£85
351–500 cc	£500	£450	£300	£200	£100
501–600 cc	£600	£600	£450	£275	£150
601 cc plus	£700	£700	£500	£325	£175

			Third-party, fire & theft		
Age	**16/17**	**18/19**	**20/21**	**22/24**	**25+**
Mopeds	£45	£35	£25	£20	£20
51–100 cc	£55	£45	£35	£30	£20
101–250 cc	£160	£155	£120	£70	£40
251–350 cc	£180	£165	£130	£75	£60
351–500 cc	£225	£205	£145	£105	£65
501–600 cc	£275	£275	£215	£145	£95
601 cc plus	£330	£330	£250	£180	£120

London, Liverpool and Glasgow – above plus approximately 25%.
Northern Ireland – above plus 100%.
The premiums shown are for standard risks, and subject to satisfactory completion of a proposal form.

Example
An 18-year-old has a 350 cc bike and would pay £390 per year for comprehensive insurance or £165 for third-party, fire and theft insurance.

Task 1
How much would these motorcyclists have to pay for insurance?
(a) A 16-year-old with a moped: comprehensive.
(b) A 28-year-old with a 600 cc bike: comprehensive.
(c) A 21-year-old with a 175 cc bike: third-party, fire and theft.

Figure 2 A vehicle licence

Vehicle excise duty

This is sometimes called vehicle licence or road tax (Figure 2). Figure 3 shows the rates for different vehicles. For motorbikes there are different rates for bikes up to and including 150 cc, between 150 cc and 250 cc, and above 250 cc.

Figure 3 Rates of vehicle excise duty

V108

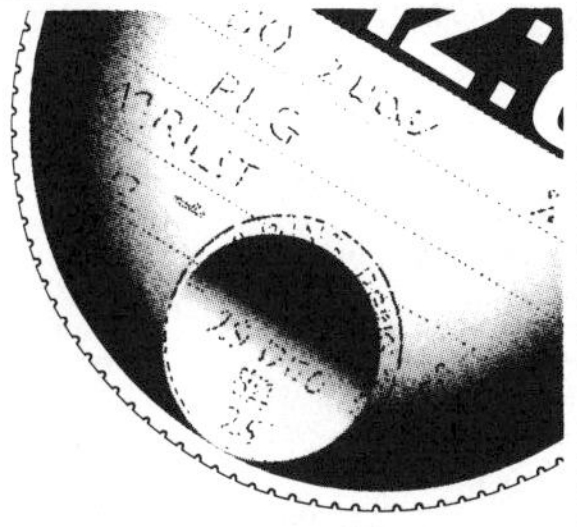

Rates of duty for motor vehicle licences

with effect from 20 March 1985

	12 months	6 months
Private/Light Goods	**£100.00**	**£55.00**
Motor Cycles		
Up to 150cc	**£ 10.00**	**-**
151 to 250cc	**£ 20.00**	**-**
Over 250cc	**£ 40.00**	**£22.00**
Tricycles		
Up to 150cc	**£ 10.00**	**-**
Over 150cc (including 3 wheeled cars not over **450** Kg)	**£ 40.00**	**£22.00**

Rates of duty for lorries and other vehicles are listed in leaflet V149 which is available at this office

Example
A 19-year-old with a 175 cc bike:

Third-party, fire and theft insurance	£155
Excise duty	£ 20
	£175 per year

Task 2
What is the total annual cost of insurance and duty for these motorcyclists?
(a) A 16-year-old with a 50 cc moped: third-party, fire and theft insurance.
(b) A 23-year-old with a 175 cc bike: comprehensive insurance.
(c) A 26-year-old with a 500 cc bike: comprehensive insurance.
(d) A 19-year-old with a 500 cc bike: third-party, fire and theft insurance.

Example
The motorcyclist in the example above works out her weekly costs on insurance and duty.

The amount per week is £175 ÷ 52
That's approximately £200 ÷ 50 = £4/week
or, using a calculator, £175 ÷ 52 = £3.3653846/week
= £3.37/week (to the nearest penny)

Task 3
What are the *weekly* insurance and vehicle-licence costs for the motorcyclists above? Work out an approximate answer first. Then use a calculator.

More about insurance

If you live in certain areas (Figure 4), insurance costs more. Using the premiums shown in Figure 1, insurance in London, Liverpool and Glasgow costs 25% extra.

That's $25\% = \frac{25}{100} = \frac{1}{4}$: one-quarter more.

In Northern Ireland, it costs an extra 100% – in other words, the cost is doubled.

Figure 4 Areas with high insurance premiums

Example
Insurance normally costing £250 would in London cost an extra quarter: ¼ × £250 = £62.50. The total cost would be £312.50.

Task 4
What would the following insurances cost?
(a) A 20-year-old with a 79 cc bike, living in Glasgow: comprehensive insurance.
(b) A 22-year-old with a moped, living in Northern Ireland: third-party, fire and theft.

(c) A 26-year-old with a 500 cc bike, living in London: third-party, fire and theft.
(d) A 17-year-old with a 175 cc bike, living in Liverpool: comprehensive insurance.

No-claims discount (NCD)

This discount is available to motorcyclists who have *not* made any claim during the year before. The discount varies from company to company. The insurance company in our example offers 10 per cent.

No-Claims Discount

A discount of 10% will be allowed where you can produce evidence of having earned NCD under a previous motorcycle insurance.

That's $10\% = \frac{10}{100} = \frac{1}{10}$: one-tenth discount.

Example
For insurance normally costing £105, the 10% discount is

$$\frac{1}{10} \times £105 = £10.50.$$

Thus the insurance *with* NCD costs £105 − £10.50 = £94.50.

Task 5
How much would these insurances cost with NCD of 10%?
(a) A 19-year-old with a 400 cc bike, living in Bristol: third-party, fire and theft.
(b) A 22-year-old with a 175 cc bike, living in Manchester: comprehensive insurance.
(c) A 17-year-old with a moped, living in Northern Ireland: comprehensive insurance.
(Does it matter which you do first – add the 100% extra for location, or take off the 10% NCD? Do it both ways to see!)
(d) A 24-year-old with a 600 cc bike, living in Liverpool: comprehensive insurance.
(e) A 20-year-old with a 79 cc bike, living in Northern Ireland: third-party, fire and theft insurance.

IMPORTANT

Read these information pages
D Percentages
F Approximations
J Calculator

2 Can I afford it?

AIM

To develop your skills in
- converting one currency to another, to varying degrees of accuracy
- applying the most appropriate conversion rate in different situations

Introduction

'Can I afford it?' is a question most of us ask ourselves at one time or another. To get an answer, we might have to look carefully at some figures, even work out a budget. This need not always be to the last penny – often an estimate will do.

Holidays

A holiday is often the single most expensive item on anyone's annual budget. It can be difficult to estimate the full cost of a package holiday: you are bound to need spending money for all those things the package doesn't cover, such as some meals, liquid refreshment, postcards home and so on. If your holiday is not a package, you have to budget for travel, accommodation and all your meals, as well as the things already listed; budgeting then becomes a real headache. Perhaps that is why package holidays have become so popular! Still, it is possible to make a fair estimate of your holiday costs by using information like that given in Figure 1. Up-to-date information like this can be found in travel agencies and in travel guides in libraries.

The first problem with budgeting is that costs are given in local currency. So the exchange rate with the pound must be found. Most newspapers publish exchange rates regularly, and they are displayed in many banks. You want the 'bank sells' column: the 'bank buys' column is for customers changing foreign currency and traveller's cheques into pounds (something you may have to do on your return). Figure 2 gives a typical example.

Example

£50 could be exchanged for $50 \times 25.40 = 1270$ Austrian schillings.

Task 1

Using Figure 2, work out how much you would be given in the foreign currency if you changed the following amounts.

(a) £100 for Maltese pounds.
(b) £100 for Moroccan dirham.
(c) £50 for Italian lire.
(d) £80 for French francs.
(e) £120 for Spanish pesetas.

Figure 1 Approximate costs of holiday items in different countries (unit of currency in brackets)

	Austria (schilling)	France (franc)	Greece (drachma)	Italy (lire)	Malta (Maltese pound)	Morocco (dirham)	Portugal (escudo)	Spain (peseta)
Simple meal out for 2	200	100	600	18 000	6.50	35	700	800
Inexpensive double room	380	80	900	25 000	10	30	900	1 000
Cup of coffee	20	4.50	50	850	0.25	3	20	65
Half-litre of beer	18	4.50	75	1 500	0.20	8.50	55	70
Cup of tea	14	5	50	600	0.19	3	25	60
Soft drink	16	8	40	900	0.19	3.50	38	65
Sun oil	57	20	300	5 800	2.12	10.50	380	380
Camera film	66	23	470	4 100	1.80	30	400	530
Postcard & postage	8	3.75	25	500	0.11	1.50	38	32
Car hire (1 week)	2 500	1 100	16 000	200 000	34.50	1 700	12 000	12 600
Petrol (per litre)	10	5	62	1 180	0.22	4.85	85	82

Figure 2 Exchange rates

Tourist Exchange Rates
We sell at

Austria	25.40
Belgium	74.00
Canada	1.5850
Rep. of Ireland	1.1725
France	11.1100
W. Germany	3.6200
Greece	150.50
Italy	2238.00
Malta	0.585
Portugal	189.00
Spain	202.25
Sweden	10.33
Switzerland	2.9750
USA	1.2000

Morocco about 11.7 (but you can't buy Moroccan currency in the UK)

You can find out up-to-date exchange rates if you have a television with ORACLE or CEEFAX

P169 CEEFAX 169 Wed 31 Oct 16:49/53
2/2
TRAVEL
Currency rates for tourists

National Westminster Bank approximate banknote selling rates for October 31st

Japan	297.00	yen
Malta	0.576	pounds
New Zealand	2.45	dollars
Norway	10.62	kroner
Portugal	193.00	escudos
South Africa	2.24	rand
Spain	204.75	pesetas
Sweden	10.44	kronor
Switzerland	2.99	francs
Turkey	475.00	lira
USA	1.205	dollars
West Germany	3.65	marks
Yugoslavia	246.00	dinars

How much is foreign money worth?

Example

£1 = 100p. This is equivalent to 25.40 Austrian schillings.

$$25.40 \text{ schillings} = 100\text{p}$$

$$1 \text{ schilling} = \frac{100}{25.40}\text{ p}$$

$$1 \text{ schilling} = 3.9370079\text{p (using a calculator)}$$

$$1 \text{ schilling} = 4\text{p (to the nearest penny)}$$

Task 2

Work out the approximate value (to the nearest penny) of:

(a) 1 French franc
(b) 1 Maltese pound
(c) 1 Moroccan dirham
(d) 2 Portuguese escudos (what's a good approximation for 1 escudo?)
(e) 100 Italian lire

Examples

1 Spanish peseta is approximately ½p.
One litre of petrol (in Spain) costs 82 pesetas: that is 82 × ½p = 41p (approx.).

100 Italian lire is approximately 4p.
Half a litre of beer (in Italy) costs 1500L: that is 15 × 4p = 60p.

Task 3

Work out the approximate costs of these items abroad:

(a) A soft drink in Portugal.
(b) A cup of coffee in Malta.
(c) A film for your camera in Italy.
(d) A week's car hire in France.
(e) Half a litre of beer in Morocco.

Task 4

(a) Choose a country and work out the costs in pounds and pence for all the items given in Figure 1.
(b) Choose an item and calculate its cost in pounds and pence in each of the countries given in Figure 1.
(c) The flow chart in Figure 3 shows how you might go about choosing a package holiday. Using your own brochures, choose a holiday and work out the total cost. You will need to include travel to and from the airport, the package price, holiday insurance, as well as extra meals and refreshments, and so on. Work out the complete travel itinerary. Present your chosen holiday in such a way that it would encourage others to join you! (You can collect some up-to-date brochures from a travel agent.)

Figure 3 Choosing a package holiday

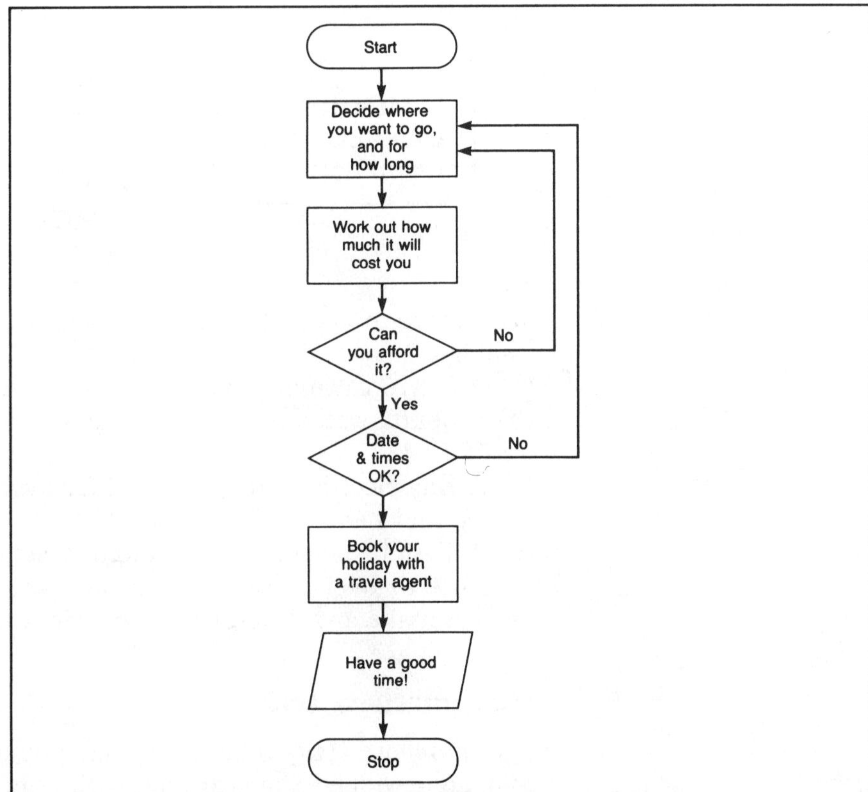

IMPORTANT

Read these information pages
B Decimals
F Approximations
J Calculator

3 Getting to grips with credit

AIM

To develop your skills in
- using tables of figures as an aid to calculation
- practising basic number skills in credit calculations
- choosing the best means of credit for various situations

Introduction

If you buy on credit you get the goods before you have paid for them in full. You have to promise to pay up eventually, of course, and you end up paying extra for the money-lending service provided. But the 'buy now, pay later' method is becoming an increasingly popular method of purchasing goods. Here are a few of the ways it can be done:
(a) through a catalogue;
(b) by hire purchase;
(c) using a credit card; and
(d) with a bank loan.

Catalogues

People who are too busy to trail round the shops often use catalogues and buy on credit. They select their goods from a catalogue, order them by post, and then pay for them weekly after the goods have arrived.

Mail order

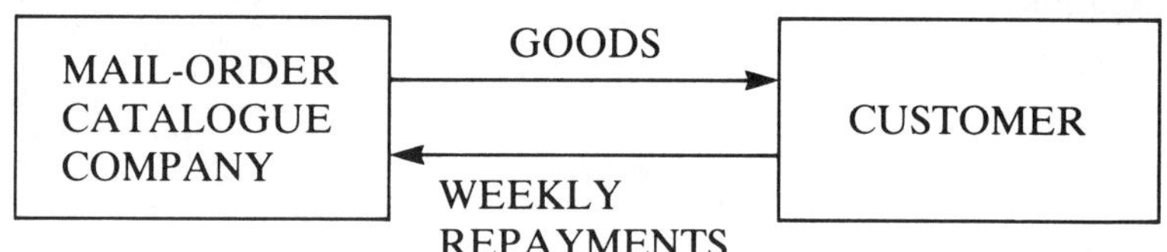

Task 1

What is the total purchase price for each of these items selected from a catalogue?
(a) A Sanyo calculator paid for over 20 weeks @ 35p per week?
(b) A quartz watch paid for over 20 weeks @ £4.00 *or* over 38 weeks @ £2.11?
(c) A Kay electric lead guitar paid for over 20 weeks @ £6.50 *or* over 38 weeks @ £3.43?
(d) A Toshiba personal stereo radio cassette paid for over 20 weeks @ £3.00 *or* over 38 weeks @ £1.58?

Does it make any difference if you repay over 20 or 38 weeks?

Hire purchase (HP)

Hire purchase (HP) is becoming less popular these days but it is still used quite widely. Shops arrange with a finance company to supply the

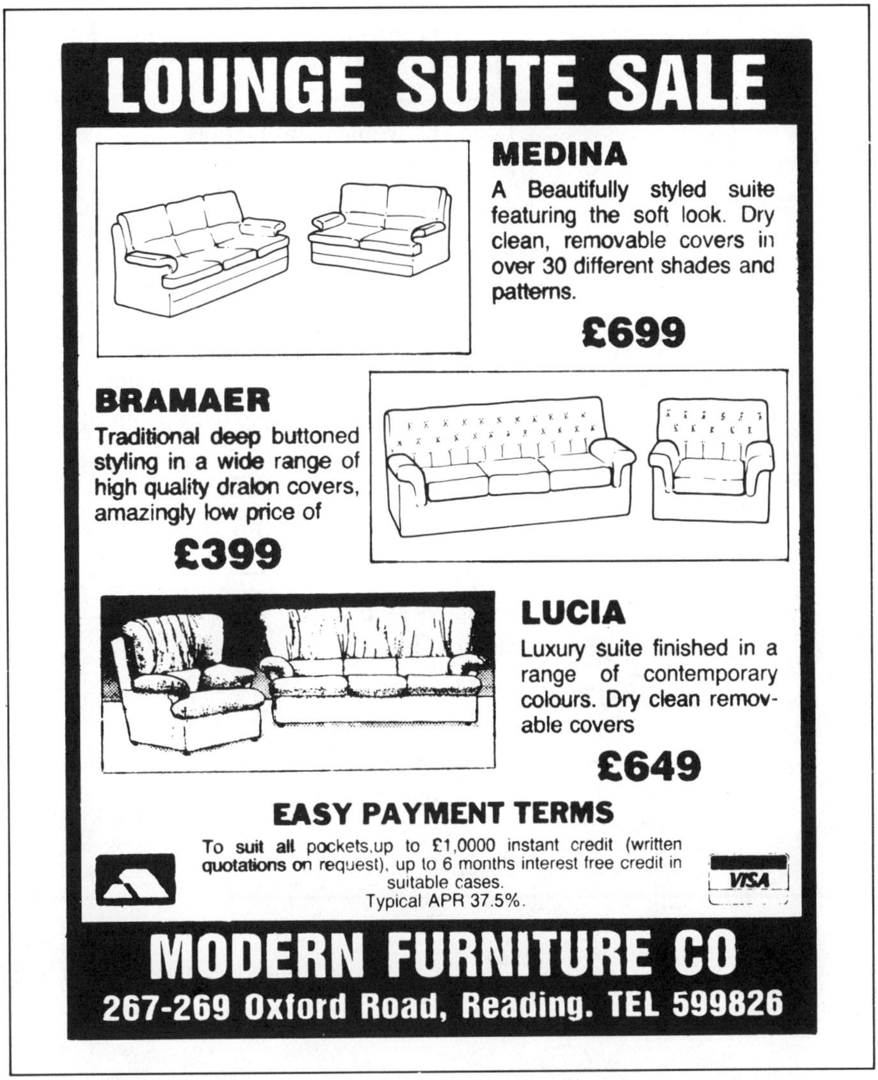

LOUNGE SUITE SALE
MEDINA
A Beautifully styled suite featuring the soft look. Dry clean, removable covers in over 30 different shades and patterns.
£699
BRAMAER
Traditional deep buttoned styling in a wide range of high quality dralon covers, amazingly low price of
£399
LUCIA
Luxury suite finished in a range of contemporary colours. Dry clean removable covers
£649
EASY PAYMENT TERMS
To suit all pockets,up to £1,0000 instant credit (written quotations on request), up to 6 months interest free credit in suitable cases.
Typical APR 37.5%.
VISA
MODERN FURNITURE CO
267-269 Oxford Road, Reading. TEL 599826

money for a purchase and the customer repays the finance company. The total repayment has to be more than the original cost of the goods, otherwise the finance company would make no profit. HP is used for large purchases (you can't buy jeans or records on HP), and technically the finance company owns the goods until the debt has been paid off.

Hire purchase

GOODS
SHOP
PAYMENT
CUSTOMER
FINANCE COMPANY
REPAYMENT INSTALMENTS

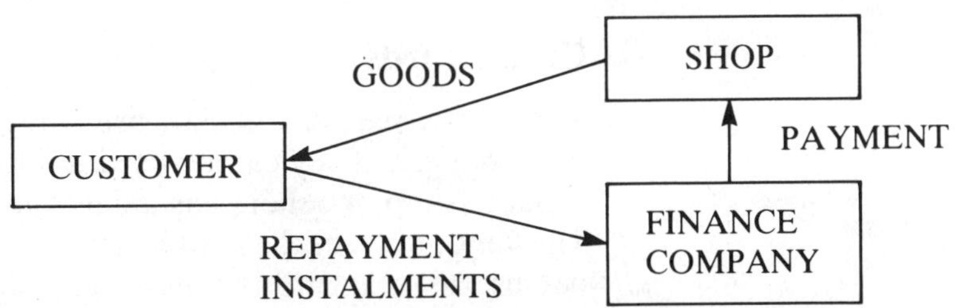

Hire purchase is available to under 18s only if guaranteed by their parents

To buy something on hire purchase you have to fill out quite a long application form. It will include personal details and a section like this:

Loan and Repayment Details	
Cost of Goods	£.......
Less Deposit	£.......
Amount of Loan	£.......
Credit Charges	£.......
Total Amount Payable	£.......
Repayments over	.... months
.... Consecutive Monthly Instalments of £.......	

Example: Buying a colour TV on HP

Loan and Repayment Details		*Notes:*
Cost of Goods	£299.00	Cash price £299
Less Deposit	£ 29.00	Initial payment £29
Amount of Loan	£270.00	299 − 29 = 270
Credit Charges	£121.56	These are worked out by the shop, but see later APR section (page 21)
Total Amount Payable	£391.56	
Repayments over	36 months	36 months, in this case – but it could be shorter or longer
36 Consecutive Monthly Instalments of £10.88		391.56 ÷ 36 = 10.876667 (using a calculator)

Task 2
Fill out the loan and repayment details for the purchase of a camera. The cash price is £119.99. An initial payment of £12 is made. Credit charges are £40.57. The repayments are over 24 months.

Credit cards

These little pieces of plastic are being used more and more widely in place of cash. They can be used to buy almost anything as long as the vendor (shop or seller) has an account with the credit-card company. The vendor places the card in a machine which imprints the customer's details on a form, the customer signs the form and the deal is complete. Every month the customer receives a bill from the credit-card company, showing all the transactions made. The customer then has the choice of paying fully or spreading the payments over a few months. For the latter service the customer pays interest: a percentage of the bill added on to it.

Credit cards

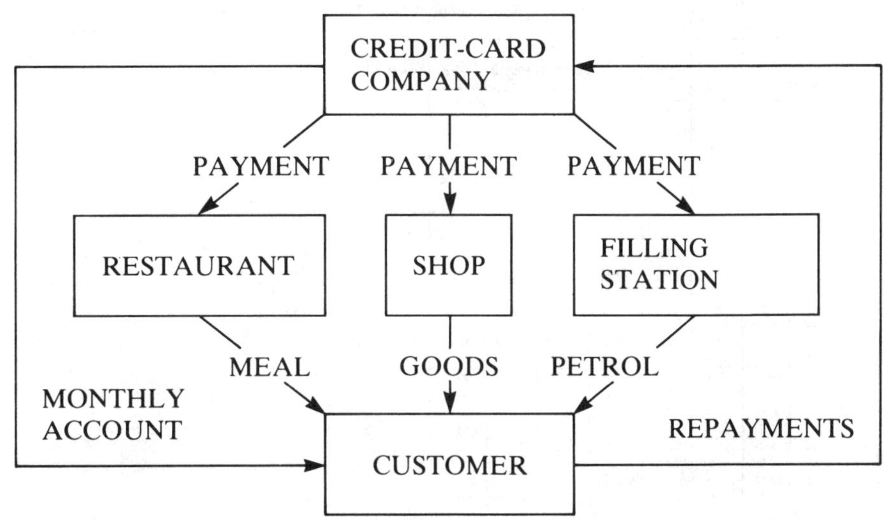

Credit cards are not generally available to people under 18

The retailer pays a percentage of the transaction to the credit-card company: this is not shown on the diagram.

Bank loans

Another important way of buying something without having to pay cash immediately is to take out a personal loan from a bank. The bank will want to know what the customer intends to buy, and may make conditions or even refuse the loan. If it agrees, the bank will transfer the money to the customer's current account; then the item can be purchased, probably with a cheque. Anyone with a bank account can apply for a personal loan.

Bank loan

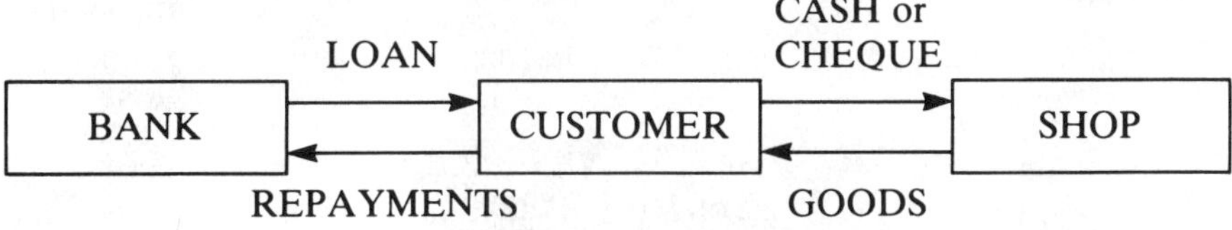

Banks will only give loans to their account holders, and will want a guarantee from the parents of people under 18

Examples

From the table shown in Figure 1, a loan of £500 over 30 months will require repayments of £20.83 monthly. This includes £124.90 in loan interest.

When calculating the repayments on a loan of £1340 it may be helpful to break it down into loans of £1000, £300 and £40, and add together the repayments for each of these:

Figure 1 Personal loan repayments

INTEREST 10% per annum flat

PERSONAL LOAN REPAYMENT TABLES

EXCLUDING ACCIDENT, SICKNESS AND UNEMPLOYMENT INSURANCE

	12 Months Annual Percentage Rate of Charge **19.62%**			18 Months Annual Percentage Rate of Charge **19.87%**			24 Months Annual Percentage Rate of Charge **19.82%**			30 Months Annual Percentage Rate of Charge **19.70%**			36 Months Annual Percentage Rate of Charge **19.47%**			48 Months Annual Percentage Rate of Charge **19.15%**			60 Months Annual Percentage Rate of Charge **18.76%**		
Amount	Total Interest	Monthly Payment	Total Amount Payable	Total Interest	Monthly Payment	Total Amount Payable	Total Interest	Monthly Payment	Total Amount Payable	Total Interest	Monthly Payment	Total Amount Payable	Total Interest	Monthly Payment	Total Amount Payable	Total Interest	Monthly Payment	Total Amount Payable	Total Interest	Monthly Payment	Total Amount Payable
£	£	£	£	£	£	£	£	£	£	£	£	£	£	£	£	£	£	£	£	£	£
10	1.04	0.92	11.04	1.52	0.64	11.52	2.00	0.50	12.00	2.60	0.42	12.60	2.96	0.36	12.96	3.92	0.29	13.92	5.00	0.25	15.00
20	1.96	1.83	21.96	3.04	1.28	23.04	4.00	1.00	24.00	4.90	0.83	24.90	5.92	0.72	25.92	7.84	0.58	27.84	10.00	0.50	30.00
30	3.00	2.75	33.00	4.56	1.92	34.56	6.00	1.50	36.00	7.50	1.25	37.50	8.88	1.08	38.88	12.24	0.88	42.24	15.00	0.75	45.00
40	4.04	3.67	44.04	6.08	2.56	46.08	8.00	2.00	48.00	10.10	1.67	50.10	11.84	1.44	51.84	16.16	1.17	56.16	20.00	1.00	60.00
50	4.96	4.58	54.96	7.42	3.19	57.42	10.00	2.50	60.00	12.40	2.08	62.40	15.16	1.81	65.16	20.08	1.46	70.08	25.00	1.25	75.00
60	6.00	5.50	66.00	8.94	3.83	68.94	12.00	3.00	72.00	15.00	2.50	75.00	18.12	2.17	78.12	24.00	1.75	84.00	30.00	1.50	90.00
70	7.04	6.42	77.04	10.46	4.47	80.46	14.00	3.50	84.00	17.60	2.92	87.60	21.08	2.53	91.08	27.92	2.04	97.92	35.00	1.75	105.00
80	7.96	7.33	87.96	11.98	5.11	91.98	16.00	4.00	96.00	19.90	3.33	99.90	24.04	2.89	104.04	31.84	2.33	111.84	40.00	2.00	120.00
90	9.00	8.25	99.00	13.50	5.75	103.50	18.00	4.50	108.00	22.50	3.75	112.50	27.00	3.25	117.00	36.24	2.63	126.24	45.00	2.25	135.00
100	10.04	9.17	110.04	15.02	6.39	115.02	20.00	5.00	120.00	25.10	4.17	125.10	29.96	3.61	129.96	40.16	2.92	140.16	50.00	2.50	150.00
200	19.96	18.33	219.96	30.04	12.78	230.04	40.00	10.00	240.00	49.90	8.33	249.90	59.92	7.22	259.92	79.84	5.83	279.84	100.00	5.00	300.00
300	30.00	27.50	330.00	45.06	19.17	345.06	60.00	15.00	360.00	75.00	12.50	375.00	89.88	10.83	389.88	120.00	8.75	420.00	150.00	7.50	450.00
400	40.04	36.67	440.04	60.08	25.56	460.08	80.00	20.00	480.00	100.10	16.67	500.10	119.84	14.44	519.84	160.16	11.67	560.16	200.00	10.00	600.00
500	49.96	45.83	549.96	74.92	31.94	574.92	100.00	25.00	600.00	124.90	20.83	624.90	150.16	18.06	650.16	199.84	14.58	699.84	250.00	12.50	750.00
600	60.00	55.00	660.00	89.94	38.33	689.94	120.00	30.00	720.00	150.00	25.00	750.00	180.12	21.67	780.12	240.00	17.50	840.00	300.00	15.00	900.00
700	70.04	64.17	770.04	104.96	44.72	804.96	140.00	35.00	840.00	175.10	29.17	875.10	210.08	25.28	910.08	280.16	20.42	980.16	350.00	17.50	1050.00
800	79.96	73.33	879.96	119.98	51.11	919.98	160.00	40.00	960.00	199.90	33.33	999.90	240.04	28.89	1040.04	319.84	23.33	1119.84	400.00	20.00	1200.00
900	90.00	82.50	990.00	135.00	57.50	1035.00	180.00	45.00	1080.00	225.00	37.50	1125.00	270.00	32.50	1170.00	360.00	26.25	1260.00	450.00	22.50	1350.00
1000	100.04	91.67	1100.04	150.02	63.89	1150.02	200.00	50.00	1200.00	250.10	41.67	1250.10	299.96	36.11	1299.96	400.16	29.17	1400.16	500.00	25.00	1500.00
2000	199.96	183.33	2199.96	300.04	127.78	2300.04	400.00	100.00	2400.00	499.90	83.33	2499.90	599.92	72.22	2599.92	799.84	58.33	2799.84	1000.00	50.00	3000.00
3000	300.00	275.00	3300.00	450.06	191.67	3450.06	600.00	150.00	3600.00	750.00	125.00	3750.00	899.88	108.33	3899.88	1200.00	87.50	4200.00	1500.00	75.00	4500.00
4000	400.04	366.67	4400.04	600.08	255.56	4600.08	800.00	200.00	4800.00	1000.10	166.67	5000.10	1199.84	144.44	5199.84	1600.16	116.67	5600.16	2000.00	100.00	6000.00
5000	499.96	458.33	5499.96	749.92	319.44	5749.92	1000.00	250.00	6000.00	1249.90	208.33	6249.90	1500.16	180.56	6500.16	1999.84	145.83	6999.84	2500.00	125.00	7500.00

To use these tables select the amount you would like to borrow, anything from £400 to £5,000 in steps of £10. (Add the figures together if the exact amount you need is not shown.) Then, you can read off the total interest, annual rate of charge, the relevant monthly payment and the total amount payable.

Where this leaflet is provided in response to a request for a quotation it does not constitute an offer and the information provided applies only on the date of receipt.

	Loan	Repayments over 48 months	Total amount payable
	1000	29.17	1400.16
	300	8.75	420.00
	40	1.17	56.16
Total	1340	39.09	1876.32

Task 3

Calculate the monthly repayments for the following loans:
(a) £600 over 36 months;
(b) £450 over 12 months;
(c) £1060 over 60 months; and
(d) £1520 over 48 months.
What is the total amount payable in each case?

Cost of loan

The cost of a loan is easy to calculate. You simply subtract the cash price of the item from the total repayments.

Example: Colour TV on HP
Cash price is £299

Deposit		£29.00
36 payments of	£10.88 =	£391.68
Total		£420.68

Cost of loan: £420.68 − £299 = £121.68.

Task 4
Work out the cost of the loans in Tasks 1, 2 and 3.

The calculations you have just made might make you think that buying from a catalogue is the cheapest form of credit – the cost of the loan seems to be £0.00 each time! However, catalogue prices are generally quite a bit higher than shop prices; the cost of the loan is already included in the catalogue price.

Annual percentage rate (APR)

It is difficult to compare one loan with another. There are two things to consider:
(a) the cost of the loan (credit price − cash price); and
(b) the length of time over which repayments are spread.
Unless one or other of these is the same for both loans, you have to find out the annual percentage rate (APR). Fortunately, loan companies are obliged to display their APR nowadays.

The APR is the percentage cost of the loan calculated over a year. So, for example, 28% APR means that a loan of £100 would cost £28 if you paid it all back a year later. The smaller the APR, the cheaper the cost of the loan. So a loan at 34.2% APR is more expensive than one at 28% APR.

Task 5
(a) A Ferguson black-and-white portable TV from a catalogue costs either £3.38 per week for 20 weeks, or £1.78 per week for 38 weeks.
  - Work out an approximation for the total cost from the catalogue.
  - Work out the exact total costs.

In the newspaper you see an advertisement for the same model for £44.95 in cash.

Figure 2 Same goods – different prices. On the left are the terms offered in a catalogue, on the right the price in a newspaper advertisement

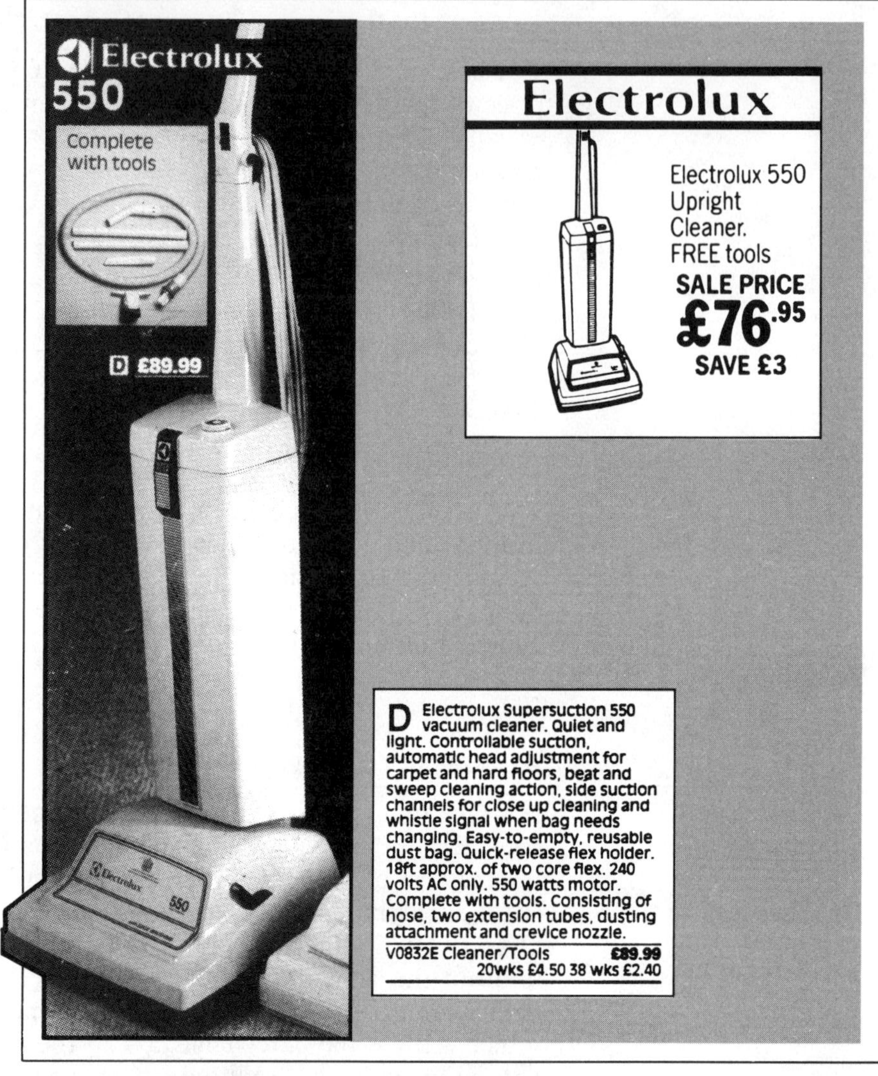

- Work out the total cost to you if you made a £4.95 deposit and took a £40 loan from the TSB.

Is this method of payment cheaper or more expensive than purchase from the catalogue?

(b) In the catalogue a Sanyo music centre may be paid for over 20 weeks @ £6.50/week, or over 38 weeks @ £3.43/week.

- What are the approximate total costs?
- What are the exact total costs?

The newspaper advertises the same item for £59.95.

- Would it be cheaper or more expensive to buy the music centre using a £60 loan from the TSB rather than to buy it from the catalogue?

IMPORTANT

Read these information pages
B Decimals
J Calculator

4 Cost of living

AIM

To develop your skills in
- doing percentage-change calculations
- drawing graphs
- comparing different methods of showing inflation

Introduction

This book was written in September and October 1984, and no doubt by the time you read it a lot of the examples will be out of date. Tax changes may have been made by the government, currency exchange rates will have altered, wages and prices will probably have gone up.

'Inflation' is the name given to the way the value of money decreases. Looking at it another way, the *rate* of inflation is the speed at which prices are increasing.

Inflation

Figure 1 shows what £1 could buy in years gone by. From this table you can see that in 1914 you could buy 94 loaves for one pound, so a loaf of

Figure 1 The purchasing power of £1

	1914	1920	1933	1947	1952	1962	1970	1983
BREAD (loaves)	94	45	72	56	39	19	11	2.25
MILK (pints)	240	107	160	107	40	30	20	4.8
POTATOES (pounds)	353	126	305	217	126	65	60	10
TEA (4 oz. packets)	53	28	44	28	21	12	13	3
BEER (pints)	80	48	34	18	16	14	9	1.5
POST (number of letters)	240	120	160	96	80	60	60	8
COAL (cwt.)	16	14.8	14.8	5.5	2.6	1.3	1.25	0.2
PETROL (gallons)	5.7	12.5	12.5	8.7	4.8	4	3	0.6

bread in those days cost

$$\begin{aligned} & £1 \div 94 \\ &= 100\text{p} \div 94 \\ &= 1.0638298\text{p (using a calculator)} \\ &= 1\text{p (to nearest penny)} \end{aligned}$$

Task 1

Find the cost of the following, to the nearest penny.
(a) One pound of potatoes in 1962.
(b) 1 cwt. of coal in 1933.
(c) 1 cwt. of coal in 1983.
(d) 4 oz. of tea in 1920.
(e) 4 oz. of tea in 1933.
What do you notice about the change in the cost of tea between 1920 and 1933?

A pound's buying power, as you can see, has in general got less and less. However, between 1920 and 1933 some prices went down. During these years there was what was known as the Great Depression. Unemployment became very high, wages were cut (see Figure 2) and people had much less money to spend. So, in many cases, manufacturers had to cut their prices in order to sell their goods.

In Task 1 you should have found that 1 cwt. of coal cost approximately 7p in 1933, and £5 fifty years later. This is an increase of £4.93 – a big increase, you might think. However, if our example had been a car and the price had increased by £4.93 over fifty years, that would be a different matter: that would seem a tiny increase.

A more useful method of expressing price change is to quote the *percentage* increase or decrease. ('Percentage' is often shortened to 'per cent' or '%'.) This can be calculated using this simple formula:

$$\text{percentage change} = \frac{(\text{new cost} - \text{original cost})}{\text{original cost}} \times 100\%$$

So in our coal example (all amounts given in £),

$$\begin{aligned} \text{percentage change} &= \frac{(5.00 - 0.07)}{0.07} \times 100\% \\ &= \frac{4.93}{0.07} \times 100\% \\ &= 7042.8571\% \text{ (using a calculator)} \\ &= 7000\% \text{ (to 2 sig. fig.)} \end{aligned}$$

Coal has increased in price by seven thousand percent over fifty years.

Example

The cost of posting a letter in 1933 was 100 ÷ 160 = 0.625p. In 1983 this had risen to 100 ÷ 8 = 12.5p.

$$\text{percentage increase} = \frac{(12.5 - 0.625)}{0.625} \times 100$$
$$= \frac{11.875}{0.625} \times 100$$
$$= 1900\% \text{ (using a calculator)}$$

Inland postage has increased in price by just under two thousand per cent in fifty years.

Task 2

Calculate the percentage increase of these items between 1933 and 1983:

(a) beer;
(b) milk;
(c) tea; and
(d) petrol.

Wages

Price increases do not necessarily mean that people are less well off. There may also have been wage rises (Figure 2).

Figure 2 Average weekly wages

	1914	1920	1933	1947	1952	1962	1970	1983
Wage	£2	£3.75	£3.50	£5.75	£9.25	£16.25	£33.50	£134.25

It is useful to indicate how well off the average person is. One way of doing this is to work out what this person could buy with his or her weekly wage.

In 1914 people could buy 2 × 240 = 480 pints of milk with their wage. In 1970 they could buy 33.50 × 20 = 6700 pints (that's nearly a thousand bottles a day!). Although there has been a large price increase over this time, the average person is better off as far as milk-drinking is concerned. In other words, the *real* cost of milk has decreased.

Task 3

(a) Using Figures 1 and 2, compare the *real* costs of these items in 1914 and 1983:
- bread
- potatoes; and
- post.

(b) Choose one or two items and show on a graph the purchasing power of the average wage-earner.

House prices

Figure 3 Average house prices

	1914	1920	1933	1947	1952	1962	1970	1983
Price	£350	£600	£650	£2 200	£2 750	£4 500	£6 500	£26 800

Figure 3 shows how the price of an average house has increased. In 1914 the average wage-earner would have taken $350 \div 2 = 175$ weeks to buy a house, not counting any interest charges on a loan.

Task 4
How long would it take an average earner to buy a house in:
(a) 1933;
(b) 1962; and
(c) 1983?

Retail price index (RPI)

Nobody in their right mind would spend all their weekly income on milk, or any other single item for that matter! Nor would they be able to use it all to pay off a loan on a house purchase. So, in order to gain an overall impression of prices at any time, it is best to use a 'shopping-basket' approach. The Retail Price Index (RPI) does just this, comparing the price of a selection of goods and services from year to year. Figure 4 gives the RPI from 1915 to 1984. If the 'shopping basket' (see later for a fuller description) cost £100 in 1974, it would have cost £19.80 in 1924 and £342.60 in 1984.

Task 5
Draw a line graph to show the change in the RPI from 1915 to 1984.

Another way of looking at it is this: a 'typical' item costing £1 (100p) in 1974 cost 19.8p in 1924 and 342.6p in 1984. So how many of these 'typical' items could a person earning the average wage buy? In 1962 they could buy

$$\frac{1625}{52.1} \text{ items (the average wage in pence, divided by the RPI)}$$

$= 31.190019$ items (using a calculator)
$= 31$ items (to 2 sig. fig.)

Task 6
Work out the purchasing power of the average weekly wage for the

Figure 4 The Retail Price Index (January 1974 = 100)

Year (January)	RPI	Year (January)	RPI	Year (January)	RPI
1915	12.5	1939	17.0	1963	53.5
1916	15.0	1940	21.9	1964	54.6
1917	18.3	1941	27.5	1965	57.1
1918	20.9	1942	28.5	1966	59.6
1919	24.5	1943	28.3	1967	61.8
1920	25.1	1944	28.3	1968	63.4
1921	29.5	1945	29.0	1969	67.3
1922	21.4	1946	29.3	1970	70.6
1923	19.9	1947	31.3	1971	76.6
1924	19.8	1948	32.7	1972	82.9
1925	20.1	1949	34.1	1973	89.3
1926	19.4	1950	35.3	1974	100.0
1927	19.5	1951	36.5	1975	119.9
1928	18.7	1952	40.0	1976	147.9
1929	18.6	1953	41.3	1977	172.4
1930	18.5	1954	41.9	1978	189.5
1931	17.0	1955	43.1	1979	207.2
1932	16.4	1956	45.1	1980	245.3
1933	15.8	1957	46.7	1981	277.3
1934	15.8	1958	48.4	1982	310.6
1935	15.9	1959	49.3	1983	325.9
1936	16.4	1960	49.3	1984	342.6
1937	16.8	1961	49.9		
1938	17.7	1962	52.1		

years 1914, 1920, 1933, 1947, 1952, 1970 and 1983. (In other words how many 'typical' items could the wage buy?) Put your answers in table form. Comment on your findings.

More about the RPI

Every month, on a certain Tuesday, hundreds of Department of Employment staff go out to survey prices in shops all over Britain. At the same time the costs of other things such as postage and rents are also recorded. Altogether 150 000 prices of 350 different items are collected, and the work begins to turn this mass of data into a single index.

First, the average price of each of the 350 items is calculated. Then the cost of the 'typical' shopping basket is worked out. The 'basket' is made up of a certain proportion of each of the items. These proportions are decided by the way the average household in the UK actually does spend its money. Household expenditure surveys are carried out regularly to find out the proportions. The proportions change over the

Figure 5 The percentage proportion, or weighting, of categories in the RPI

	1968	1975	1983
Food	26.3	23.2	20.3
Alcoholic drink	6.3	8.2	7.8
Tobacco	6.6	4.6	3.9
Housing	12.1	10.8	13.7
Fuel and light	6.2	5.3	6.9
Durable household goods	5.9	7.0	6.4
Clothing and footwear	8.9	8.9	7.4
Transport and vehicles	12.0	14.9	15.9
Miscellaneous goods	6.0	7.1	7.5
Services	5.6	5.2	6.3
Meals out	4.1	4.8	3.9
Total	100.0	100.0	100.0

years; for instance, people smoke less nowadays, so cigarettes and tobacco now take up a smaller proportion of the 'basket'. Another example is that a colour TV is now considered part of the average household's budget, whereas only a few years ago it was not included in the RPI.

The RPI covers rents, rates, transport and services as well as retail goods, so perhaps the name 'Consumer Price Index' would be better. It does not include things like income tax and national-insurance contributions, even though these affect most people's living costs.

Figure 5 shows the proportions of the 350 items in the basket in 1968, 1975 and 1983, if they were grouped in eleven broad categories.

IMPORTANT

Read these information pages
F Approximations
G Charts and graphs
J Calculator

Task 7

(a) Draw pie charts to illustrate the proportions of each category found in the RPI shopping basket for the years 1968, 1975 and 1983.

(b) Discuss why there have been changes over the years.

5 Tax

AIM

To develop your skills in
- calculating percentages of amounts of money
- displaying information in pie charts
- solving tax problems through calculation

Introduction

People in Britain have suffered taxation for at least a thousand years. The Domesday Book was drawn up in 1086 in order to give King William I (William the Conqueror) tax and census information. Since then there have been head taxes, horse taxes and window taxes, amongst others.

Nowadays, there are two main collectors of taxes, the Board of Inland Revenue and the Board of Customs and Excise. They collect our taxes to provide central government with its funds. The Inland Revenue collects income tax, national-insurance contributions and other forms of direct taxation, taxing people's wages and incomes, business deals and transactions. Customs and Excise collect the indirect taxes on goods and services. VAT or value-added tax is the main one of these, but there is also separate taxation of beer, wine, spirits, petrol and tobacco.

Income tax

Income tax is the major source of income for central government. Most people pay income tax under a scheme called PAYE which stands for Pay As You Earn. It just means that the income tax is spread out over the tax year rather than having to be paid in a lump sum. The tax year runs from 6 April of one year to 5 April of the next. During this time, a person is allowed to earn a certain amount of money which is not taxed at all, called an *allowance* or *free pay*. Under PAYE this allowance is spread out weekly or monthly.

A person's free-pay allowance is indicated by their tax code. These are the two most common (based on figures for 1985):

Status	**Tax Allowance** (per year)	**Code**
Single person	£2005	200L
Married person*	£3115	315H

* Only one of a couple can claim the married person's allowance: the other will have a single person's allowance.

Task 1

(a) How much per week is the single person's allowance? How much per month?

(b) How much per week is the married person's allowance? How much per month?

The *standard* rate of income tax is 30 per cent. You can earn £15 400 per year on top of your personal allowance before a *higher* tax rate becomes payable.

Example

A single person (with code 200L) earning £6500 per year will pay tax on £6500 − £2005 = £4495. The tax rate will be 30%.

PAYE tax = 30% of £4495
= 30% × £4495
= £1348.50

So the total tax payable will be £1348.50.

Task 2

Work out how much tax, in a year, the following people would pay.

(a) Income £4800, tax code 200L.
(b) Income £5600, tax code 315H.
(c) Income £7000, tax code 315H.
(d) Income £8400, tax code 200L.
(e) Income £10 000, tax code 315H.

In Task 1 you should have calculated that the weekly tax allowance for a single person is £38.56 (to the nearest penny). Under PAYE, if this allowance is not used up, it can be carried forward to the following weeks until the end of the tax year (5 April).

For this example we will assume that no tax allowance is to be carried forward.

Example

A person with tax code 200L, earning £79.10 weekly, will pay standard-rate tax on £79.10 − £38.56 = £40.54.

Tax = 30% of £40.54
= 30% × £40.54
= £12.162
= £12.16 (to the nearest penny)

Someone receiving a monthly salary will have their tax calculated on the basis of the monthly tax allowance.

Task 3

Calculate the PAYE tax payable by the following people. Assume that there is no tax allowance to be carried forward.

(a) JR earns £78.56 per week and has tax code 200L.
(b) MH earns £332.92 per month and has tax code 315H.
(c) HC earns £300.08 per month and has tax code 200L.
(d) AT earns £120 per week and has tax code 315H.
(e) SG earns £93.50 per week and has tax code 200L.

National Insurance (NI)

National Insurance (NI) is the second greatest source of income for central government. NI contributions are collected by the Inland Revenue, along with PAYE income tax, in order to pay for retirement pensions, unemployment benefit, sick pay and so on.

Below a yearly income of £1767.96, called the lower earnings limit, an employee pays no NI contribution. Above this limit, NI is payable on the *full* income. (The lower earnings limit is *not* an allowance.) The standard rate of NI contributions is 9 per cent of full income.

Example

A person earning £6500 per year will pay 9 per cent of £6500.

1% of £6500 = £65

so 9% of £6500 = 9 × £65 = £585

This person's NI contribution will be £585 year. A person earning £1500 per year will pay no NI because this amount is below £1767.96, the lower earnings limit.

Task 4

£1767.96 is the yearly lower earnings limit.

(a) How much could you earn a week before you had to pay NI?

(b) How much could you earn a month before you had to pay NI?

Above these limits, NI is payable on the *full* income. These limits are not allowances. Work out the NI contributions on the following earnings.

(c) £72 per week

(d) £300 per month

(e) £45.45 per week

(f) £32.50 per week

(g) £138 per month

(h) £327.40 per month

Value-added tax (VAT)

Of the indirect taxes, VAT raises the most money for the government. At the moment the standard rate of VAT is 15 per cent and this is charged on most goods and services. More information on this tax will be found in Assignment 16.

Government revenue

Where does it come from? Where does it go? These are two important questions which are answered in Figure 1. Figure 1 compares income from different sources in the years 1980, 1981 and 1982. The bottom section shows how this income was spent.

Figure 1 Central government: income and expenditure, 1980–82

Income	1980	1981	1982
	£ million		
Income tax	24 279	27 637	30 272
Corporation tax	4 663	4 142	4 986
Value-added tax (VAT)	11 445	12 525	14 255
Tax and duties on petrol and oil	5 224	8 420	10 141
Duties on wines, spirits and beer	2 519	2 993	3 346
Duties on tobacco	2 696	3 166	3 540
Motor-vehicle duties and car tax	1 811	2 003	2 425
National Insurance contributions	17 442	19 654	20 880
Rent, dividends and interest	5 996	6 842	7 953
Miscellaneous	3 156	3 594	4 205
TOTAL	79 231	90 976	102 003
Expenditure			
Defence	11 334	12 547	14 350
National Health Service	10 819	12 335	13 122
Other government administration and services	7 321	8 288	9 203
Social-security benefits and pensions	21 001	25 992	30 252
Grants to local authorities	13 201	15 143	16 090
Subsidies	4 284	4 685	4 181
Debt interest	8 735	10 611	11 672
Miscellaneous	5 209	5 709	6 545
TOTAL	81 904	95 310	105 415
DEFICIT	2 673	4 334	3 412

Source: Central Statistical Office, 1983

Task 5

(a) Present a table showing Government income and expenditure for the year 1980, giving the figures rounded to the nearest 100. (Remember that the figures are in millions, so this means to the nearest 100 000 000.) Show the totals of the rounded figures. By how much do they differ from the totals in the original table?

(b) For 1982, present the figures for income and expenditure rounded to the nearest 1000. Show the totals of the rounded figures. How much do they differ from the totals in the original table?

(c) Display the figures given for 1981 in the form of two bar charts, one for income, the other for expenditure.

(d) Work out the percentage of total income for each category in 1980. *Example:* Income tax was 24 279 million pounds out of 79 231 million pounds. That is

$$\frac{24\,279}{79\,231} \times 100\% = 30.6\% \text{ (1 decimal place)}$$

Display your results in a table.

(e) Work out the percentage of total expenditure for each category. Display your results in a table.

(f) Draw two pie charts, one to show government income in 1980, the other to show expenditure. Use your answers from questions (d) and (e).

IMPORTANT

Read these information pages
G Charts and graphs
H Averages

LIVERPOOL INSTITUTE OF HIGHER EDUCATION
THE MARKLAND LIBRARY

Pay packet

AIM

To develop your skills in
- presenting the results of arithmetical problems in table form
- reading and checking a payslip
- calculating a person's net pay under PAYE

Introduction

When you start work you might be asked, or even expected, to join a trade union. It is quite likely that a trade union will negotiate your wage rates and working conditions with the management.

In order that workers can check their pay, holiday entitlement and so on, trade unions often publish and distribute to their members a leaflet detailing these wage rates and conditions. If a worker has problems he or she can then quickly consult the steward or other union representative.

Rates of pay

Figure 1 shows the 1983–84 pay rates for local-government manual workers published by the National Union of Public Employees (NUPE). The type of work determines what group the worker is in. Group A includes messengers and cleaners, Group B includes road labourers and some park attendants, Group C includes launderette attendants, D assistant cooks, E gardeners, and F driver/plant operators, for example.

Figure 1 Sample rates of pay for different workers

Grade Rates

Group	Weekly (£)	Hourly (p)
A	70.30	180.25
B	71.40	183.08
C	73.20	187.69
D	76.50	196.15
E	79.10	202.82
F	82.40	211.28
G	85.25	218.59

The above wage rates are to be used for the calculation of overtime, bonus and other similar enhancements.

Task 1

Calculate the length of the working week for each grade of workers. This can be done by dividing the weekly wage by the hourly rate. *Both* figures must be in pence (or both in pounds) before you do the division. Is the working week the same for all the groups?

Premium payments, those over and above the standard rates, are often paid on a 'time and a fraction' basis.

These are the rates for local-government manual workers:

	Rate
Overtime, Monday to Saturday	Time and a half
Overtime, Sundays	Double time
Nights	Time and a third
Split duty	5p per hour
Unsocial hours (day workers)	Time and a fifth

('Split duty' refers to a shift that is worked as two separate periods during the day.)

Example

A park attendant (Group B) is normally paid 183.08p per hour. Working overtime on a Tuesday, he or she will be paid time and a half. In other words,

pay = 183.08p plus half of 183.08p per hour
= 183.08p + 91.54p per hour
= 274.62p per hour

Task 2

Calculate the hourly rates for workers earning premium payments. Copy this table and fill in the figures you have calculated.

		Hourly rates including premium payments				
		Overtime				
Group	**Basic rate**	Mon–Sat	Sunday	**Nights**	**Split duty**	**Unsocial hours**
A	180.25					
B	183.08	274.62				
C	187.69					
D						
E						
F						
G						

Example
A park attendant (Group B), working the normal 39-hour week, does two hours overtime on Tuesday. The weekly wage for this will be

$$39 \times 183.08\text{p} = 7140.12\text{p}$$
$$2 \times 274.62\text{p} = \underline{549.24\text{p}}$$
$$\text{Total} = 7689.36\text{p}$$

Gross pay is pay before any deductions – such as income tax and national insurance – are made. The park attendant's gross pay will be £76.89.

Task 3
Work out the gross pay that the following manual workers should expect.

(a) A messenger (Group A) working a basic week plus 3 hours overtime on Saturday.
(b) A cleaner (Group A) working 45 hours, Monday to Friday.
(c) A road labourer (Group B) working a basic week and then 6 hours overtime on Sunday.
(d) A groundsman's assistant (Group C) working a basic week with 3 hours overtime on Saturday and 3 hours on Sunday.
(e) A swimming-pool attendant (Group F) working 8 hours per day, Wednesday, Thursday and Friday, 8 hours on Saturday, and 6 on Sunday.

Net pay

Gross pay is the amount you earn before deductions. *Net pay*, or *take-home pay*, is the amount after deductions have been made. The deductions will be income tax and national insurance. Other deductions, such as a union subscription, may be agreed with your employer.

Figure 2 shows a typical payslip. Income tax and national insurance are calculated as in Assignment 5.

Example
Our park attendant, Pat Johnson, has tax code 200L. Pat therefore has a weekly tax allowance of £38.56.

Income tax of 30% is taken on
£76.89 − £38.56 = £38.34.
30% of £38.34 = £11.50.

National insurance of 9% is also deducted:
9% of £76.89 = £6.92.

Pat pays union dues direct to NUPE.

Task 4
Examine Pat Johnson's payslip and check that you understand the entries and how they are calculated.

Figure 2 A payslip

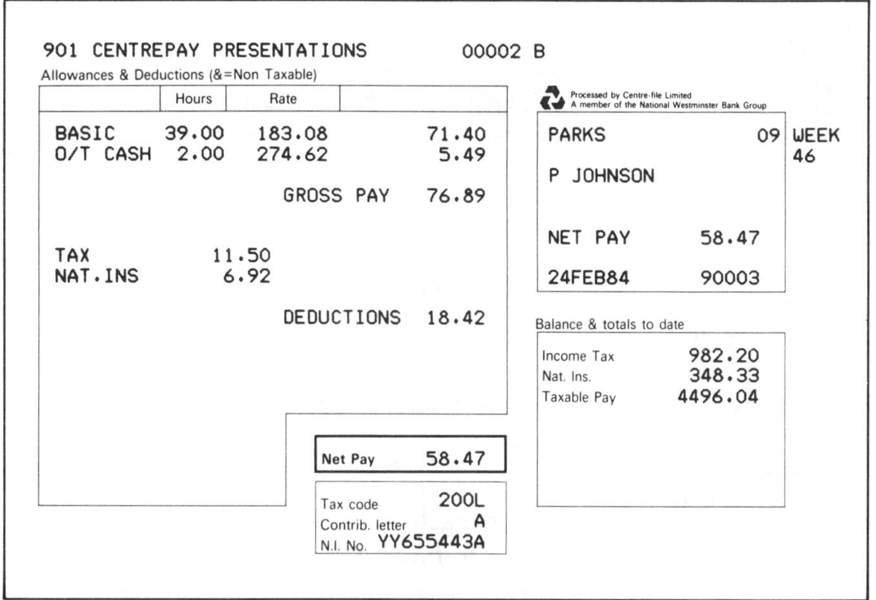

901 CENTREPAY PRESENTATIONS 00002 B

Allowances & Deductions (&=Non Taxable)

	Hours	Rate		
BASIC	39.00	183.08		71.40
O/T CASH	2.00	274.62		5.49
			GROSS PAY	76.89
TAX	11.50			
NAT.INS	6.92			
			DEDUCTIONS	18.42

Net Pay 58.47

Tax code 200L
Contrib. letter A
N.I. No. YY655443A

Processed by Centre-file Limited
A member of the National Westminster Bank Group

PARKS 09 WEEK 46

P JOHNSON

NET PAY 58.47

24FEB84 90003

Balance & totals to date

Income Tax	982.20
Nat. Ins.	348.33
Taxable Pay	4496.04

IMPORTANT

Read these information pages
C Fractions
D Percentages

For the following employees, calculate their gross pay, income tax, national insurance, total deductions and net pay. Enter the amounts as they would appear on a payslip.

(a) Les Walker is a pest-control operative (Group F) who does five hours' overtime on Saturday as well as the basic 39-hour week. Les's tax code is 315H.

(b) Jo Underhill is a launderette attendant (Group C). Jo does no overtime and has tax code 200L.

7 Room to move

AIM

To develop your skills in
- measuring lengths and angles
- determining area and volume from given dimensions
- using measurement and calculation to assess hazards at work

Introduction
An overcrowded workplace, whether it be an office, shop or factory, is a health hazard. There will be more risk of injury, greater stress for the workers, and less light.

Adequate space for working

The UK regulation minimum space for a worker is not generous by any means, yet still today there are many factories and offices that do not reach these standards.

The Factories Act requires 400 cubic feet for each worker, with no height over 14 feet above the floor to be taken into account.

Example
Consider a workshop with dimensions 30 ft. × 45 ft., and height 13 ft.

Volume = 30 × 45 × 13 cu. ft. = 17 550 cu. ft.

Maximum number of workers = 17 550 ÷ 400 = 43.875.

Therefore 43 workers could be employed in the workshop. (You do not round up to 44, because then each worker would have *less* than 400 cu. ft.)

Task 1
Calculate the maximum number of workers that can be employed in factory spaces of the following dimensions:
(a) 20 ft. × 35 ft., height 12 ft.
(b) 55 ft. × 27 ft., height 20 ft. (Remember that this has to be treated as 14 ft., as the extra 6 ft. in height cannot be taken into account.)
(c) 63 ft. × 29 ft., height 16 ft.
(d) What ceiling height or heights give the smallest legal floor space per worker? Calculate this minimum floor area per worker.

The Offices, Shops and Railway Premises Act

This Act states that each person must have at minimum 400 cu. ft. *and* at minimum 40 sq. ft. Space taken up by machinery, furniture, and fittings must not be included in this calculation.

Example
An office for 5 people must have a floor area, excluding furniture, etc., of at least 200 sq. ft.

If the ceiling is 10 ft. or higher, the volume per person will then be at least 400 cu. ft. (because 40 sq. ft. × 10 ft. = 400 cu. ft.).

However, if the ceiling is *less* than 10 ft. above the floor, more floor area will be needed per person to obtain the 400 cu. ft. If the ceiling is, say, 9 ft. high, the floor area per person should be 400 ÷ 9 = 44.44 sq. ft. (to 2 decimal places). So the 5 workers must then have 222 sq. ft. altogether (5 × 44.44 = 222.2, then round to the nearest whole number of sq. ft.).

Task 2

(a) Calculate the floor area, excluding furniture, required per person for an office with a ceiling height of:

- 8 ft.
- 8 ft. 6 in. (8.5 ft.)
- 9 ft. 6 in.
- 11 ft. 6 in.

(b) An office for 4 clerical workers measures 14 ft. by 16 ft. and the ceiling height is 11 ft. The furniture takes up an area of 55 sq. ft. Work out the area per worker. Is this adequate?

(c) A typing pool measures 28 ft. by 17 ft., with ceiling height 12 ft. 6 in. The furniture occupies an area of 100 sq. ft. Is this adequate room for the 10 typists?

(d) A general office houses 3 employees. Calculate the area per person if the room is 15 ft. square with a ceiling height of 8 ft. 6 in., and with furniture occupying 45 sq. ft. Is this adequate? Is there enough room for an extra worker to be employed in the office?

(e) The regulations are expressed in imperial units (feet) because they were set out before metrification in the UK. Convert 40 sq. ft. to square metres (m^2), and 400 cu. ft. to cubic metres (m^3).

Are you sitting comfortably?

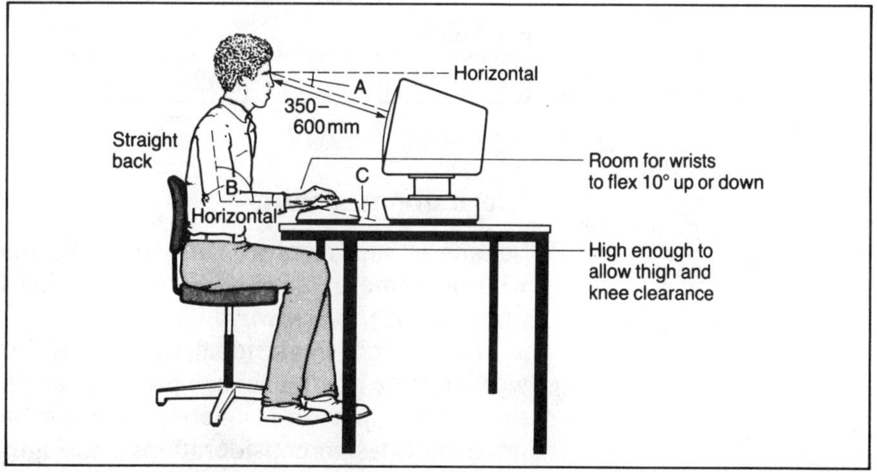

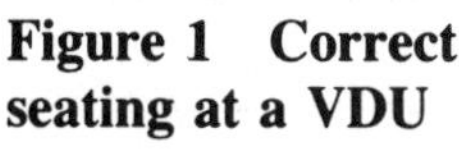
Figure 1 Correct seating at a VDU

Figure 1 shows how a VDU operator should be seated. There are some other considerations (for instance there should be room for documents to be within easy reach), but the ones shown are the main ones.

Task 3

Using a protractor, measure the angles *A, B* and *C* in the pictures in Figure 1. Copy and complete the table and comment on the seated operator's working posture (position) in Figures 1 and 2(a) to (c).

Figure 2 Other people at VDUs

Figure 2a **Figure 2b** **Figure 2c**

	Angle A	Angle B	Angle C	Comment (correctly seated?)
Figure 1				yes
Figure 2a				
Figure 2b				
Figure 2c				

More about seating

Seating is important not just for VDU operators, but for all workers who do some or all of their work sitting down. Poor postural habits often result in *permanent* damage.

There is no single ideal sitting position and it is important for a worker to be able to change position, as this relieves tiredness. A chair that holds a person in one position is a bad one. However, there are important design considerations and Figure 3 shows the main ones.

Figure 3 Designing a seat

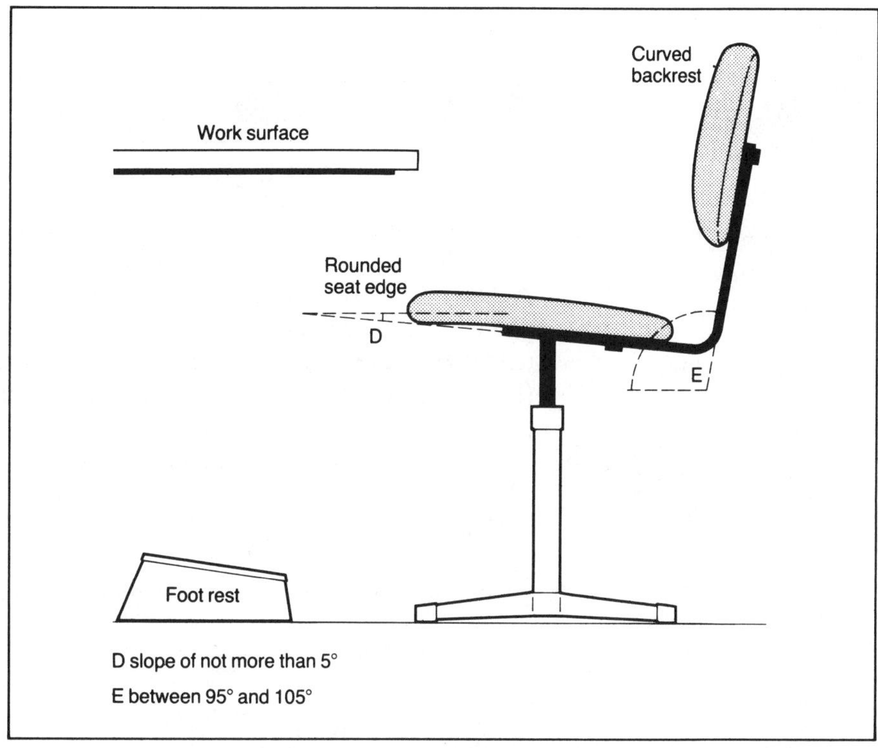

(a) A seat height of 43 cm would suit 75 per cent of men and women, but a seat that is adjustable from 34 to 52 cm is much better.
(b) A seat depth of 38 cm suits 99 per cent of men and women.
(c) The seat width should be 40 cm.
(d) The backrest should be between 20 and 33 cm above the seat.
(e) The chair arms (if any) should be 21 cm above the chair seat, and a minimum of 48 cm apart.

Task 4

(a) Measure a selection of chairs, and decide which ones are suitable for a worker. Use a checklist that starts something like this:
- Rounded seat edge? YES/NO
- Curved backrest? YES/NO
- Slope of seat: ......

(b) Convert the metric measurements given above to inches, using a calculator. 1 cm = 0.394 in.

IMPORTANT

Read this information page
E Area and volume

LIVERPOOL INSTITUTE OF HIGHER EDUCATION
THE MARKLAND LIBRARY

8 Air to breathe

AIM

To develop your skills in
- calculating areas, volumes and time-weighted averages
- appreciating the need for fresh air in the working environment

Introduction

Both the Factories Act and the Offices, Shops and Railway Premises Act say that there must be adequate fresh-air ventilation in a workplace. There are four reasons for supplying air to buildings:

(a) so that the occupants have air to breathe;
(b) to remove cigarette smoke, body odour and other smells;
(c) to keep the body temperatures of the workers at a steady level, neither too hot nor too cold; and
(d) to control contamination in the air.

It is easy to imagine the problems in these four areas in factory conditions, but the problems also exist in offices. Poor ventilation is a very common complaint made by office workers.

Natural ventilation

The regulations are not very specific, but the Institution of Heating and Ventilating Engineers recommend that there should be a minimum 5 sq. ft. of openable windows for every 100 sq. ft. of floor area. These windows can be in the walls or in the roof. Otherwise there should be mechanical ventilation.

Example

An office 12 ft. by 15 ft. has area $12 \times 15 = 180$ sq. ft. Therefore there should be at least

$$\frac{180}{100} \times 5 = 9 \text{ sq. ft. of openable window.}$$

Task 1

(a) Calculate the minimum recommended openable window area for the following:
- office: 20 ft. × 18 ft.;
- workshop: 25 ft. × 16 ft.;
- shop: 20 ft. × 21 ft.;
- factory: 112 ft. × 42 ft.; and
- mailroom: 12 ft. × 14 ft.

(b) The specification (5 sq. ft. for every 100 sq. ft.) is easily converted to metric. How much window area in square metres (m^2) should there be for every 100 m^2 floor area?

Mechanical ventilation

Many workplaces do not have adequate openable windows; some have no windows at all. In these cases mechanical ventilation is required. There are recommendations on the quantities of fresh air necessary for such spaces. Here are some of them:

Space	Level of smoking	Cubic feet per minute per person
Bank	some	10
Department store	some	10
Factory	none	10
Hospital ward	none	20
Hotel room	heavy	30
Laboratory	some	20
Office	none	25
	heavy	30
Cafeteria	heavy	12
Retail shop	none	10

Example
A hospital ward with 12 patients and 4 staff would require 16 × 20 = 320 cu. ft. per minute of ventilation.

Task 2
Calculate the ventilation required for these workspaces:
(a) A twin room in a hotel.
(b) A busy cafeteria with four workers and seating for 50.
(c) An office of five clerical workers, none of whom smoke.
(d) A factory workshop with 15 workers, in which smoking is not allowed.
(e) An office of six typists, some of whom smoke.

The third reason given for ventilation was to maintain a comfortable working temperature. This is quite a complicated issue as the best temperature is largely determined by the degree of physical effort involved in the work. Control of humidity, the amount of water in the air, is also important. This should be at a level between 30 and 70 per cent. It may be worthwhile to find out more about temperature and humidity.

Toxic fumes

In many workplaces it is possible that toxic (poisonous) fumes may get into the air – not only in factories, but in offices as well.

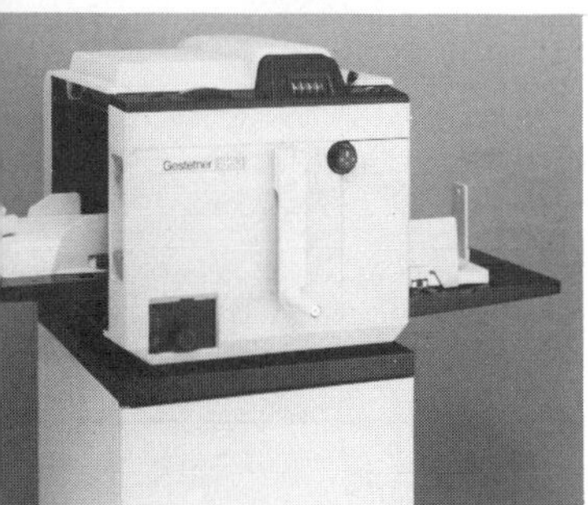

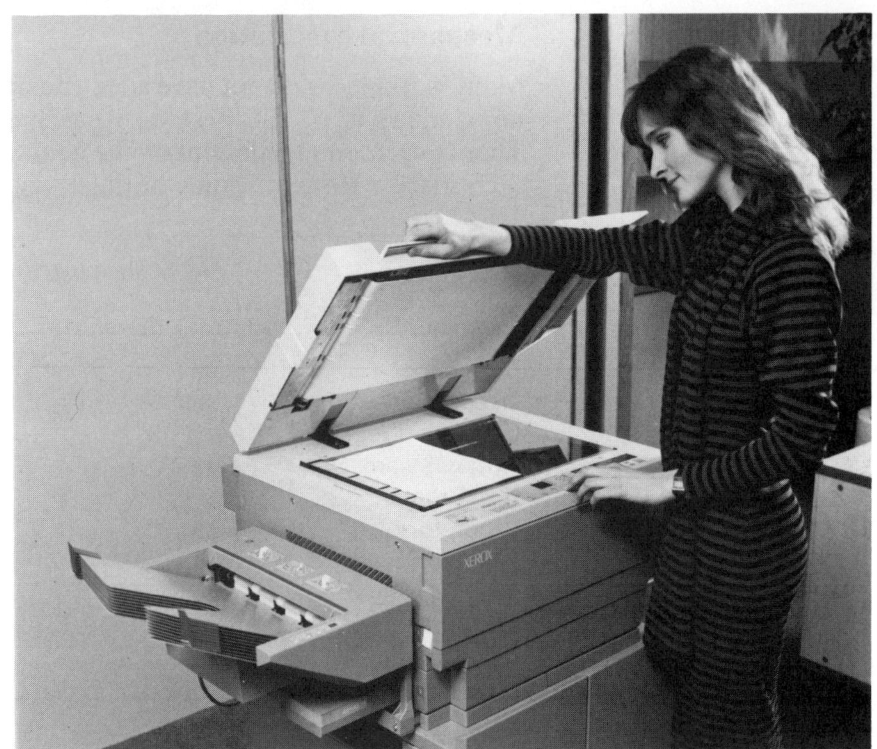

For instance, spirit duplicators and microfilm-developing equipment use ammonia; and most correction fluids, like Tippex, contain 1.1.1 trichloroethane (trike). Fumes from these could perhaps accumulate to toxic concentrations if there was poor ventilation. Trike is also widely used as a cleaning agent throughout industry. Electrostencil machines give off carbon dust and other poisonous gases such as acetic acid and acrolein. Photocopiers emit ozone, which may be sweet-smelling but which is a highly toxic gas. It is recommended that these machines should be confined to areas away from desks.

Exposure limits are recommended by the Health and Safety Executive for almost all toxic substances. Below these limits, as far as is known, there is no danger to a worker's health. Long-term exposure limits are based on the average exposure per hour, spread over an eight-hour period. This is known as an eight-hour *time-weighted average* (TWA).

The concentration of airborne substances is measured in milligrams per cubic metre of air (mg m^{-3}). (A milligram is a thousandth of a gram. Metric units are used because these are recent standards.) If this measured concentration was maintained for an eight-hour shift, then this figure would itself be given as the TWA. However, if the concentration was kept up only over a shorter period, then the TWA would have to be calculated by working out the average concentration per hour spread over eight hours.

Example
An operator works 5 hours on a process that gives off aluminium-metal dust at a concentration of 15 mg m^{-3}.

$$\begin{aligned}
\text{8-hour TWA} &= \frac{\text{time} \times \text{concentration}}{\text{eight hours}} \\
&= \frac{5 \times 15}{8}\ \text{mg m}^{-3} \\
&= 9.375\ \text{mg m}^{-3} \\
&= 9.4\ \text{mg m}^{-3}\ \text{(to 2 sig. fig.)}
\end{aligned}$$

The recommended *limit* for this substance is 10 mg m^{-3} in 8 hours, so this situation is just below the limit and therefore considered acceptable.

Task 3
What would be the 8-hour TWA in these situations? Which would not be considered acceptable?
(a) A process emits 24 mg m^{-3} ammonia fumes for 6 hours. The recommended limit for the 8-hour TWA is 18 mg m^{-3}.
(b) The level of wood dust in a furniture workshop is 4 mg m^{-3} for 4 hours. In hardwood furniture-making the recommended limit for the 8-hour TWA for wood dust is 1 mg m^{-3}.
(c) Welding fumes in a garage are at a level of 8 mg m^{-3} for 3 hours. The recommended limit for the 8-hour TWA for these fumes is 5 mg m^{-3}.
(d) In an office a photocopier emits ozone at 0.16 mg m^{-3}. It is left on for 7 hours. The recommended limit for the 8-hour TWA is 0.2 mg m^{-3}.

Often in an 8-hour shift the exposure to the toxic substance will vary.

Example
Acrolein is a gas given off by an electrostencil-cutting machine. Its long-term exposure limit is 0.25 mg m^{-3}.

Working period	Duration (hr.)	Concentration (mg m^{-3})
8.45–11.15	2.5	0.12
11.30–12.30	1.0	0.25
1.45– 4.45	3.0	0.15

$$\begin{aligned}
\text{8-hour TWA} &= \frac{2.5 \times 0.12 + 1 \times 0.25 + 3 \times 0.15}{8} \\
&= \frac{1.0}{8} \\
&= 0.125\ \text{mg m}^{-3}
\end{aligned}$$

In this case the exposure is below the recommended limit.

Task 4

Work out the 8-hour TWA in each of these examples. The recommended limit is given in brackets ($mg\,m^{-3}$).

(a) Toluene ($375\,mg\,m^{-3}$) is contained in cellulose thinner which is used in car paint-spraying.

Working period	Duration (hr.)	Concentration ($mg\,m^{-3}$)
9.00–13.00	4.0	300
14.00–17.00	3.0	400

Extract ventilation is important when this substance is being used. The dangers are of

- fire;
- poisoning (from inhalation); and
- dermatitis (from skin contact).

(b) Carbon monoxide ($55\,mg\,m^{-3}$) is present in car exhaust fumes. This gas may be a problem in workplaces like vehicle ferries, garages, repair workshops and underground car parks.

Working period	Duration (hr.)	Concentration ($mg\,m^{-3}$)
8.00– 9.00	1	75
9.00–12.00	3	50
13.00–16.00	3	45
16.00–17.00	1	85

IMPORTANT

Read these information pages

B Decimals
E Area and volume
F Approximations

Car paint spraying

Car paint spraying gives off vapours which are potentially explosive or ignitable. So you must not have any naked flame in the workroom – that means no propane-gas heaters and no smoking! It also means that normal electrical apparatus, such as light fittings, cannot be used because of the risk of sparks. Regulations zone off a workroom as in Figure 1. Special electrical equipment must be used in each zone.

Figure 1 A workroom in which cars may be spray-painted

9 Keep the noise down

AIM

To develop your skills in
- reading information from graphs
- identifying how sound is measured
- assessing the risk to health and safety from noise

Introduction

Noise is not just a nuisance; it is now recognised as a *major* health hazard, especially in industry.

People generally do not know when sound is damaging their hearing – it often doesn't hurt. Sometimes people actually enjoy loud noise, for instance at rock concerts. However, with continued exposure to loud noise, people's hearing ability gradually declines. They may also end up suffering for the rest of their lives from *tinnitus*, which is a continual ringing, rumbling and scraping sound in the ears.

Frequency and intensity

Sound is energy that reaches the ear in the form of vibrations in air pressure. There are two things that are important to understand – frequency and intensity.

The *frequency* of a sound is the number of vibrations per second. It is expressed in hertz (Hz) or sometimes in cycles per second. Imagine a stone being dropped into the middle of a pond: ripples will widen over the surface of the pond. The number of ripples created in one second corresponds to the frequency. A human ear can generally hear sound in the range 20 Hz, which is a low rumble, up to 16 000 Hz, a high-pitched squeak.

Intensity is represented by the height of the ripple above the surface of the pond. As the ripple moves, or radiates, from the centre, its height decreases, in the same way as sound intensity decreases as you move away from the source.

Intensity is, in fact, a measure of the amount of energy. Its measurement is based on the sound that the ear can only just hear – known as the threshold of hearing. If this has an intensity of 1, then the intensity of normal speech is roughly 100 000 (a hundred thousand). Other typical sounds and their approximate intensities are given in Figure 1. At very high intensities sound becomes painful: this level is known as the threshold of pain. A jet engine with intensity of 10 billion (million million) is on the threshold of pain.

A scale of sound from 1 to 10 000 000 000 000 would be very difficult to handle, and what is known as a *logarithmic scale* is generally used. This scale is based on units called decibels (dB). The way decibels correspond to sound intensity is shown in Figure 1.

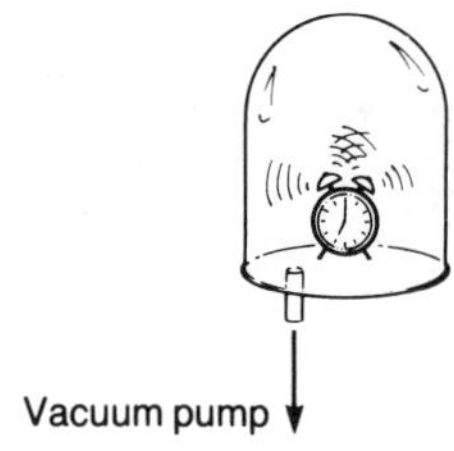

You may have seen the physics experiment in school in which a clock is placed in a large jar which is then evacuated. As the vacuum is created, the sound of the clock gets less and less. This demonstrates that sound energy travels through air. Sound energy can also pass through liquids and solids, but it cannot travel through a vacuum.

From the table in Figure 1 it can be seen that, for instance, street traffic at 80 dB is ten times stronger in intensity than the sound from a loud radio, 70 dB. Or that a jet engine, 130 dB, is 10 000 times stronger in intensity than a lathe, 90 dB. Each step of 10 dB is a sound 10 *times* stronger.

Figure 1 The scale of sound

dB	Sound intensity	Typical sounds	
0	1	threshold of hearing	
	×10		
10	10	rustle of a leaf	
	×10		
20	100	very quiet room	
	×10		
30	1 000	whispering	
	×10		
40	10 000	low radio music; quiet office; fridge hum (at 2 m)	
	×10		
50	100 000	normal speech	
	×10		
60	1 000 000	busy office	
	×10		
70	10 000 000	loud radio; car at 40 mph; noisy office with typewriters	
	×10		
80	100 000 000	street traffic; inside moving tube train	risk range
	×10		
90	1 000 000 000	heavy machinery; lathes; HGV from pavement	risk range
	×10		
100	10 000 000 000	noisy indoor swimming pool; sheet-metal shop, pneumatic drills	risk range
	×10		
110	100 000 000 000	woodworking shop; rock drill	deafness range
	×10		
120	1 000 000 000 000	boiler shop; diesel-engine room; disco (1 m from loudspeaker)	deafness range
	×10		
130	10 000 000 000 000	jet engine; riveting	deafness range

The decibel (dB) is one tenth of a bel. The 'bel' unit was named after Alexander Graham Bell, the inventor of the telephone.

Task 1

How much stronger in sound intensity is:

(a) a pneumatic drill than a busy office?
(b) normal speech than whispering?
(c) a busy office than a very quiet room?
(d) a woodworking shop than a sheet-metal shop?
(e) a diesel-engine room than a jet engine?

You might be thinking that normal speech doesn't *seem* a hundred times louder than whispering. This is because your ear itself operates on a logarithmic scale. A 10 dB increase sounds only like a doubling to the ear, although it is ten times the pressure on the eardrum.

An increase of 10 dB means that the sound intensity is multiplied ten times. A doubling of sound intensity is an increase of only 3 dB (3.01, to be a little more accurate). So if a pneumatic-drill operator is alone and without ear protection, he or she would experience 100 dB. Two drill operators side by side would experience 103 dB, four operators together would experience 106 dB, and so on.

More about frequency and intensity

A pure note, played on a musical instrument perhaps, has one frequency. If you recorded the note, you could then play it back at a number of different sound intensities. The frequency would remain the same at the different volumes.

However, most sound is made up of a large number of different frequencies, and it is the higher frequencies that are potentially more hazardous. Special noise meters are designed to concentrate on those frequencies that have an effect on the human ear. These are calibrated on a scale called db(A), which operates exactly like the decibel scale described before.

Task 2

Graph A in Figure 2 shows at what sound intensity someone would just begin to hear sounds – the threshold of good hearing – at different frequencies. Read off the sound intensity for this threshold at these frequencies:

(a) 2000 Hz
(b) 250 Hz
(c) 125 Hz
(d) 8000 Hz
(e) 500 Hz

Figure 2 Sound levels

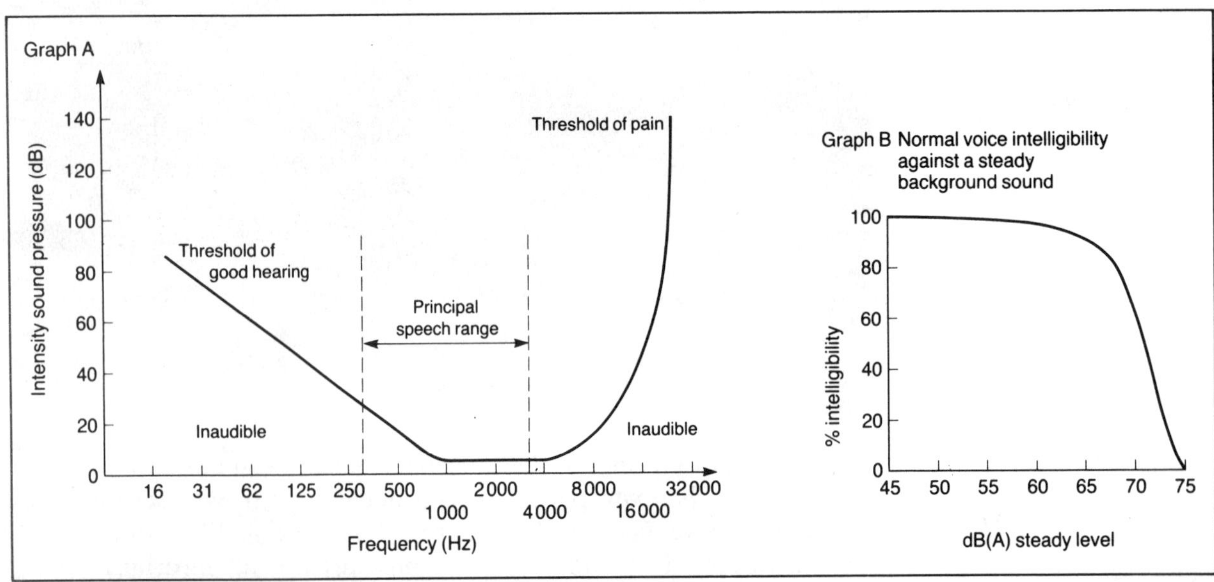

Usually when there is a steady background noise our hearing threshold is raised. In other words, hearing sound above the background becomes more difficult. Graph B shows how well normal speech can be understood against a steady background level, in say a typical living room or office. Where there is a steady background noise people generally raise their voices to be understood clearly. However, where noise regularly gives rise to problems in communication and where clear communication is necessary in the interest of safety, people may have to learn to lip-read or use other visual signs.

Task 3

Read off from the graph the percentage intelligibility at these steady dB(A) levels:

(a) 55
(b) 60
(c) 65
(d) 70
(e) 75

A person whose hearing has been damaged often cannot hear sounds of a frequency higher than 400 Hz. Consequently their hearing of speech is distorted: they miss the 's', 't' and 'f' sounds.

A number of regulations have been laid down to reduce the threat to thousands of workers' hearing. It is estimated that there are between one and two million people who suffer from hearing loss as a result of noise at work.

The regulations

A worker can be exposed to a maximum level of 90 dB(A) for an eight-hour day. The sound level can only be increased if the time is reduced. 93 dB(A) is twice the sound intensity of 90 dB(A), so this level can only be maintained for four hours. Two hours is the maximum exposure for sound levels of 96 dB(A), and so on.

Task 4

Copy and complete the table below.

Max. sound level in dB(A)	Exposure limit per day
90	8 hr.
93	4 hr.
96	2 hr.
99	1 hr.
102	⋮
⋮	⋮ } work in minutes and seconds
135	

135 dB(A) is the absolute maximum level of exposure

If the sound level is changing – for instance sometimes at 99 dB(A), sometimes at 90 dB(A), sometimes 85 dB(A) – a more complicated calculation has to be made to check that the level does not exceed the basic 90 dB(A) over eight hours.

In the regulations it is assumed that no damage can be caused by levels below 85 dB(A), but this is disputed by many experts. Above 85 dB(A) protective equipment should be provided, and shop stewards should insist on it. Up to 105 dB(A) ear plugs will probably be sufficient. Ear muffs are suitable up to 115 dB(A). Above this, noise-protection helmets are necessary.

IMPORTANT

Read this information page

G Charts and graphs

10 Drawn to scale

AIM

To develop your skills in
- understanding the concept of scale in a map or plan
- converting measurements on a scale drawing to life-size

Introduction

Figure 1 shows an architect's drawings for a proposed new house. Before any building can be put up, architects have to submit drawings to the council for planning permission. The drawings show the plans of the building, as though looking from above. The architect also has to submit a map of the site and a map of the general area, called the location plan. A full set of drawings would also include views of front, back and sides, called elevations, and a cross-section through the building.

Obviously the drawings cannot be full-size. Paper doesn't come that big. So all the dimensions are scaled down.

Scale

Look at Figure 1. The location plan is to the scale 1 : 2500. This means that every distance on the map is 1/2500 of the real distance. In other words, if you measure a distance on the plan and multiply it by 2500 you will get the distance in real life.

If the other drawings were done to this scale, they would be tiny.

For instance the house would be about this big – no good for any detail. A different scale needs to be chosen so that the necessary detail can be seen in the drawing. The site plan in Figure 1 is drawn at 1 : 500 to show the house in relation to the other houses around. The plan, the front, back and side elevations, as well as the cross-section views, are drawn at 1 : 100 because much more detail has to be shown.

Example

Look at the ground-floor plan. The living room is 4.4 m long.

$4.4\,\text{m} = 4400\,\text{mm} \; (1\,\text{m} = 1000\,\text{mm})$

On a scale 1 : 100, the drawing will be 1/100 of life-size.

$$\frac{1}{100} \times 4400\,\text{mm} = 44\,\text{mm}$$

Check that the plan of the living room is 44 mm long.

The living room measures 28 mm wide on the plan. The scale is 1 : 100, so the real room will be 100 times the plan size. The width of the living room will be

$$100 \times 28\,\text{mm} = 2800\,\text{mm} = 2.8\,\text{m}$$

Figure 1

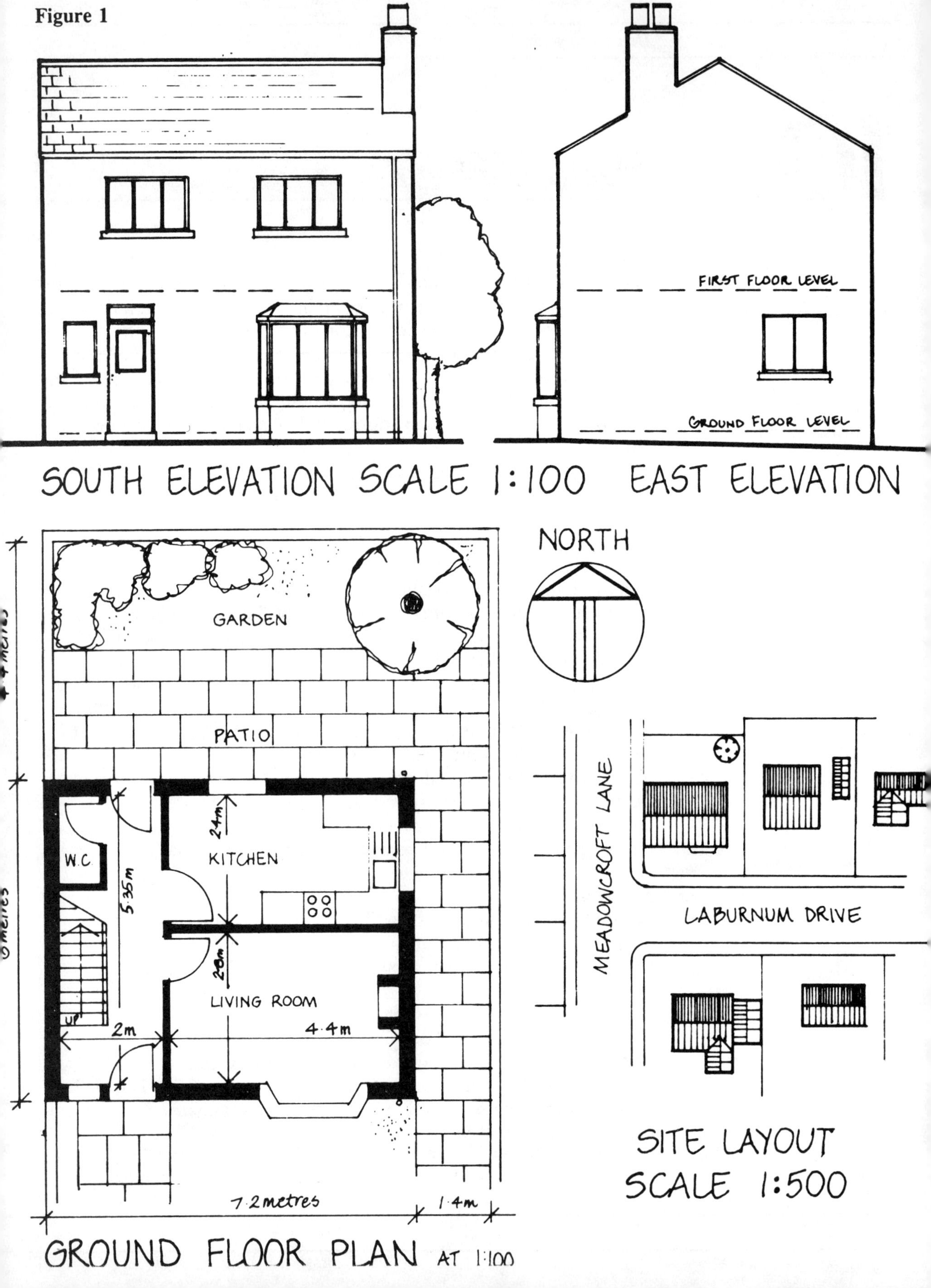

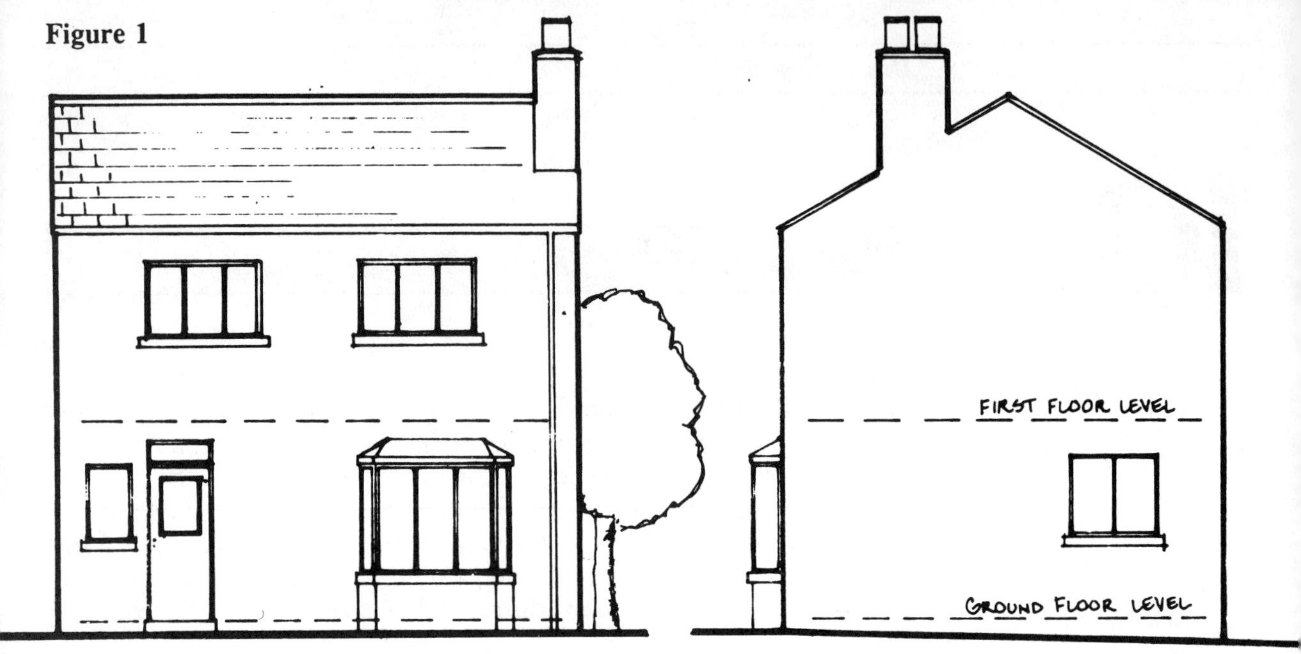

FIRST FLOOR LEVEL
GROUND FLOOR LEVEL
SOUTH ELEVATION SCALE 1:100
EAST ELEVATION
GARDEN
PATIO
W.C.
KITCHEN
LIVING ROOM
UP
2.4m
5.35m
2.8m
2m
4.4m
7.2metres
1.4m
GROUND FLOOR PLAN AT 1:100
NORTH
MEADOWCROFT LANE
LABURNUM DRIVE
SITE LAYOUT
SCALE 1:500

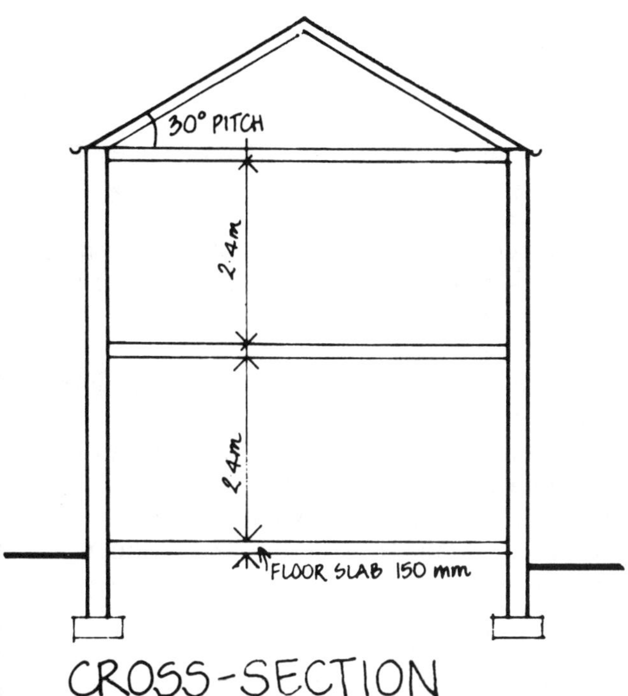

CROSS-SECTION

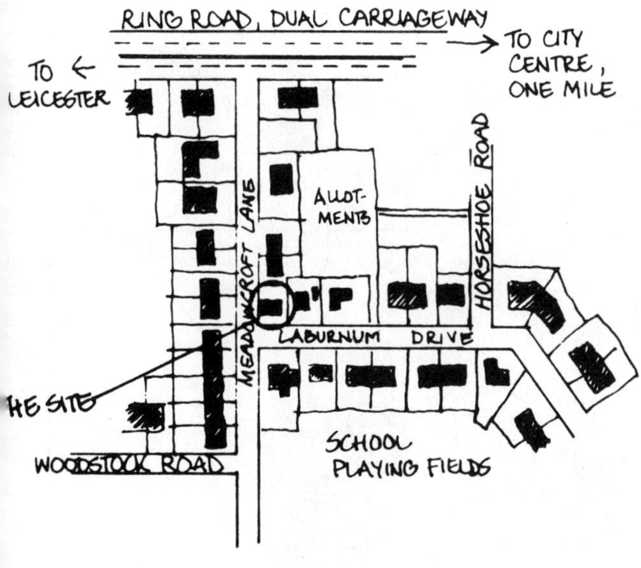

LOCATION PLAN
SCALE 1:2500

GENERAL NOTES:

MATERIALS TO BE USED:
BLUE SLATE ROOF
DARK RED BRICK WALLS, SOUTH, WEST & EAST ELEVATIONS, & CHIMNEY STACK.
CONCRETE RENDER TO NORTH WALL, PAINTED BUFF COLOUR, 08 B 17 (BRITISH STANDARD 4800 NUMBER).
HARDWOOD WINDOWS, STAINED DARK.

NOTE: THIS IS NOT A WORKING DRAWING — FOR PLANNING APPLICATION ONLY

PROPOSED NEW HOUSE AT 59, LABURNUM DRIVE FOR J.S. DANBY.

SCALES:	DATE:	DRAWN BY:
1:100, 1:500 & 1:2500	OCT '84	HR.

H.R. ARCHITECTS
RIPON, N. YORKSHIRE
TELEPHONE: 602 5934

Task 1

Use Figure 1.

(a) On the plan, measure the dimensions of the WC. Calculate the length and width of the real WC.

(b) How wide will the corridor on the ground floor be?

(c) The patio is an upside-down L shape. Measure its dimensions carefully, then calculate its size in real life. Draw a sketch of the patio and mark on these dimensions. (You will need this for Task 2.)

(d) On the site layout, measure the distance to the house next door. The scale is 1 : 500. Calculate what this distance will be in real life.

(e) On the location plan, measure the distance from the house to the dual carriageway. Calculate what this distance will actually be. The scale is 1 : 2500. How accurate do you think your result is?

(f) What is the walking distance from the front door to the allotments?

Figure 2 Paving slabs

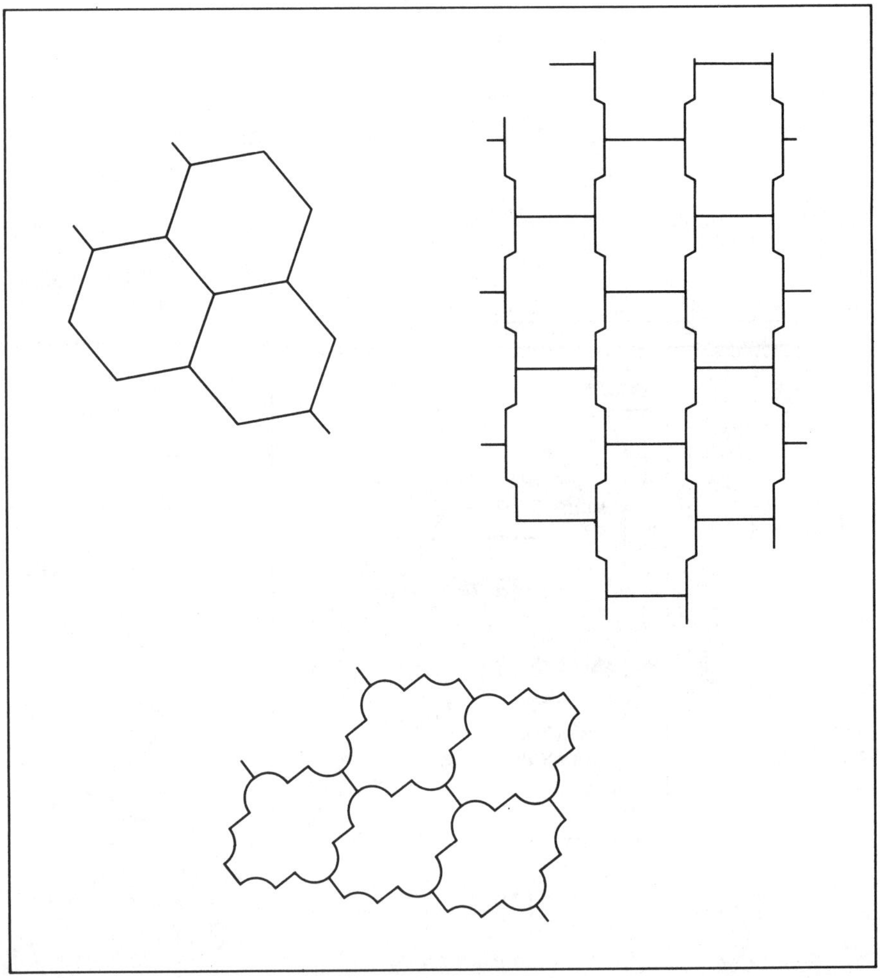

Figure 3 A complicated shape may comprise several rectangles

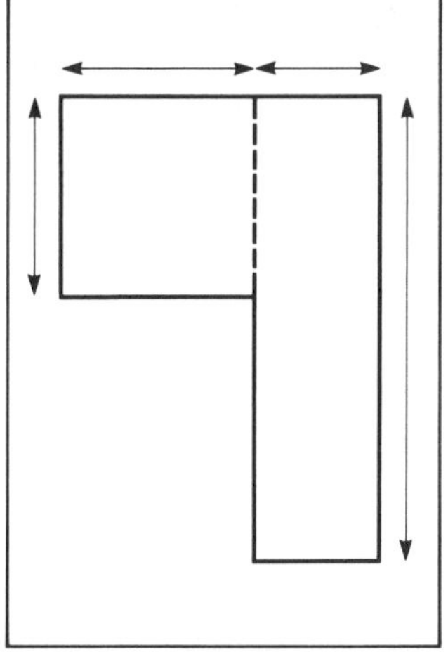

The patio in the plan has been paved using rectangular slabs. However, many shapes could be used, from squares to the more complicated shapes shown in Figure 2.

Task 2

(a) The area of the patio can be calculated by treating it as two rectangles. The area of each rectangle can be worked out, and the two results added together. Do this.

(b) If the area of one paving slab is $0.2\,m^2$, how many paving slabs would be needed to cover the entire patio?

Task 3

(a) Choose a room or workspace and measure it carefully. Make two scale drawings of it, one to fit on a postcard and the other to fit on a piece of A4 paper. State the scale used in each case.

(b) Find out the cost of replacing the floor covering of this room or space using different materials, such as carpet tiles, lino, or concrete. Which type of covering is most suitable and why?

IMPORTANT

Read this information page
E Area and volume

The photograph shows part of the computer used by a large firm of architects. The computer will display plans to whatever scale the operator wants. The right-hand screen shows part of the left-hand screen, but to a much bigger scale. The grid you can see on the right-hand screen is made up of dots that would be 300 mm apart in real life. The entire plan of the building, in this case a hospital, could have been entered into the computer by giving the co-ordinates of doors, walls, and so on, using the grid.

LIVERPOOL INSTITUTE OF
HIGHER EDUCATION
THE MARKLAND LIBRARY

Focus assignments

11 Cooking for crowds

AIM

To develop your skills in

- making conversions between the metric and imperial systems of measurement
- deciding on appropriate quantities of food required for catering

Introduction

It is Shrove Tuesday, and at the last minute a young catering assistant has been landed with the task of providing pancakes for the hotel guests. She quickly looks up a recipe and finds the following:

For 8 pancakes
4 oz. flour
½ pt. milk
½ tsp. salt
1 egg
fat for frying

Changing the quantities

There are 12 guests staying for dinner. Allowing 2 pancakes each, she needs to make 24 pancakes. She knows that 3 × 8 = 24 so she can immediately say that she needs 3 times the quantities given in the recipe.

3 × 4 = 12 oz. flour
3 × ½ = 1½ pt. milk
3 × ½ = 1½ tsp. salt
3 eggs
fat for frying

When word gets round that pancakes are on the menu, 5 more guests decide to stay for dinner. This makes a total of 17, and at two pancakes each, that means 34 pancakes to be fried. Four times the recipe quantities is not enough (4 × 8 = 32), 5 times would be too much (5 × 8 = 40 pancakes) but maybe there could be seconds.

Each time she has increased the quantities she has kept them in the same proportion to each other. The quantities are different but the *ratio* of flour to milk to egg has stayed the same.

Task 1

What ingredients would be needed for
(a) 64 pancakes?
(b) 121 pancakes?
(c) 9 pancakes?

An in-between quantity would need a fraction of an egg. However, the calculation can be done. One pancake uses ⅛ of the recipe, that is:

⅛ × 4 = ½ oz. flour
⅛ × ½ = ¹⁄₁₆th pt. milk
⅛ × ½ = ¹⁄₁₆th tsp. salt
⅛ egg
fat for frying

When catering for large numbers of people it can be difficult to guess how much food to get. A list like this (adapted from a standard catering textbook) can be used to calculate the approximate quantities needed:

Soup: 4 or 5 portions per litre
Caviar: 15–30 g per portion
Fish fillet: 8 portions per kg.

Meats
Roast beef (boneless): 6 portions per kg
Beef stew/pie: 8 portions per kg
Rump steak: 120–250 g per portion
Cold ham: 10–12 portions per kg
Chicken: 360 g per portion

Vegetables
New potatoes: 8 portions per kg
Old potatoes: 4–6 portions per kg
Other vegetables: 6–8 portions per kg

The quantities are given in two different forms, size of portion or number of portions in a given quantity.

Example
Soup yields 4 or 5 portions per litre – say 5 portions per litre (not very generous!). So for 20 portions, 20 ÷ 5 = 4 litres are required.

For caviar you need 15–30 g per portion – say 25 g. So for 20 portions you need 20 × 25 g = 500 g.

Task 2
Work out quantities of the following:
(a) roast beef for 60 people;
(b) fish fillet for 36 people;
(c) chicken for 20 people;
(d) rump steak for 25 people;
(e) cold ham for 35 people; and
(f) new potatoes for 91 people.

All the figures above use metric weights and measures. Often suppliers work in imperial units (pounds, pints, etc.) so it may be necessary to convert from one to the other.

Here are some approximate conversions:
1 kg = 2.2 lb.
1 litre = 1.75 pints
1 lb. = 0.45 kg
1 pint = 0.57 litre

Example
6 kg = 6 × 2.2 = 13.2 lb.

Task 3
Convert the following quantities:
(a) 7 kg to pounds;
(b) 8 litres to pints;
(c) 9 lb to kilograms; and
(d) 12 pt. to litres.

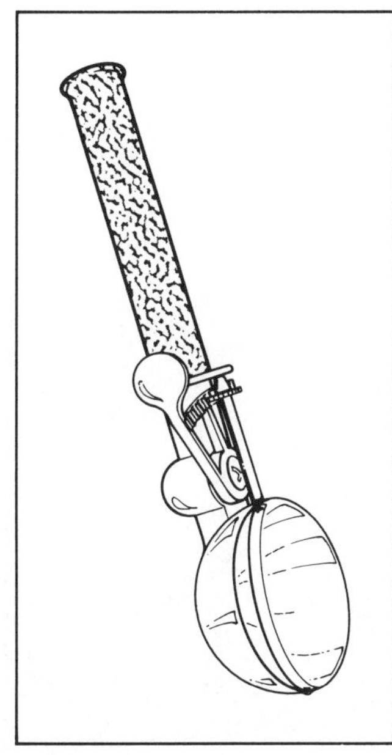

Figure 1 An ice-cream scoop

Task 4
Figure 1 shows an everyday object found in the kitchen. It uses a simple mechanical device in order to release scoops of ice cream or creamed potatoes.

Find other gadgets around the kitchen, draw them, and explain how they work. Look at whisks and garlic presses for a start.

Task 5
Figure 2 shows a flow chart for cooking egg custard. Design a flow chart for your favourite recipe.

Figure 2 Flow chart for cooking egg custard

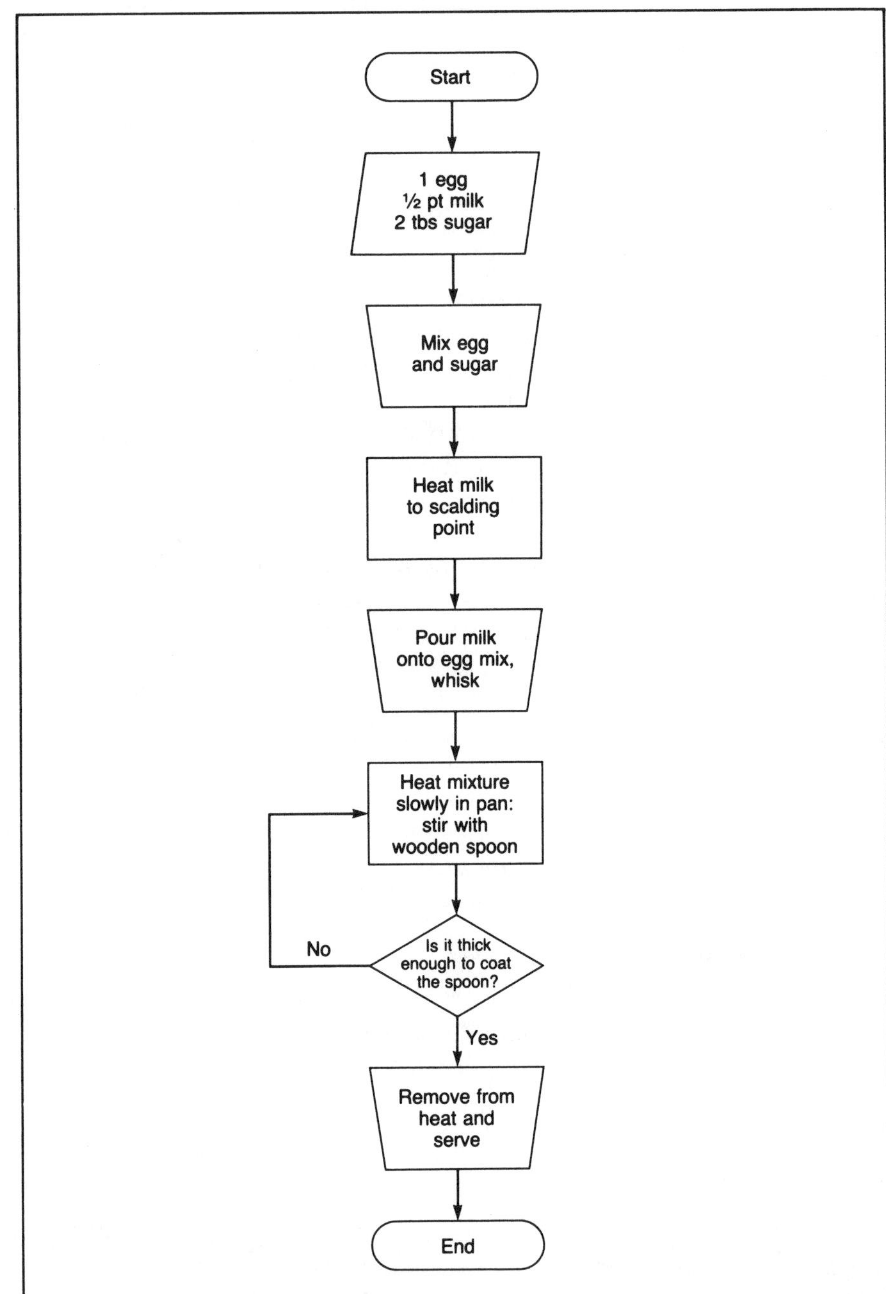

IMPORTANT

Read these information pages
B Decimals
C Fractions

12 Constructive ideas

AIM

To develop your skills in
- measuring angles
- working out areas given linear dimensions
- making safety decisions about flights of stairs or steps

Introduction

Except for builders and architects, probably few people think much about stairs, windows, and all the other details of building construction. We all tend to take them for granted.

Stairs

Before stairs are constructed in a building, a number of careful calculations have to be made. One of these concerns the pitch, or steepness, of the stairs.

The steepness can be measured by the angle of pitch. This is the angle between the pitch line (shown in Figure 1) and the horizontal. The angle of pitch should not be less than 25°, because if the stairs are too shallow, they will take up a lot of room and will be tiring to go up.

If the stairs are too steep, they will be dangerous. The angle of pitch should not be greater than 42° for a private stairway (that is, one in a home) or greater than 38° for a common stairway (one in a block of flats or offices).

Figure 1 A staircase

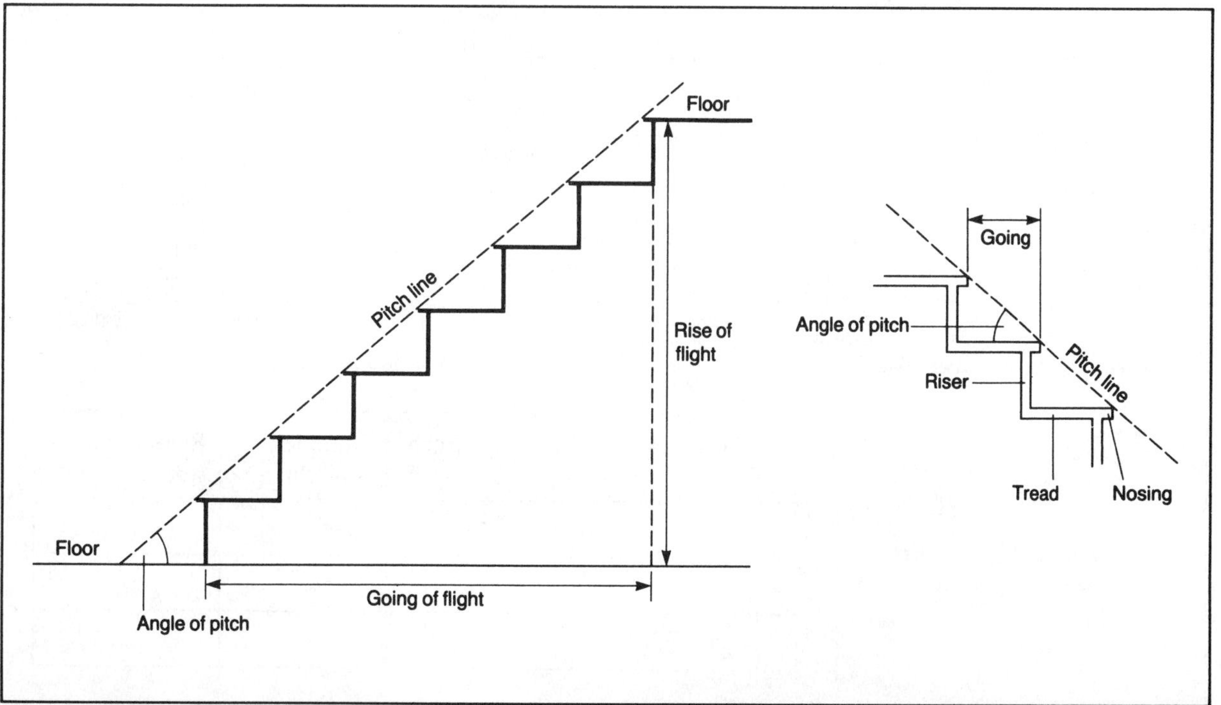

Task 1

(a) Using a protractor, measure the angle of pitch for the staircase in Figure 1. You should find that it is 40°. Would this staircase be suitable if found in an office? If not, why not?

(b) Measure the angle of pitch of the stairs in the four diagrams in Figure 2. Copy and complete the table.

Figure 2 Various staircases

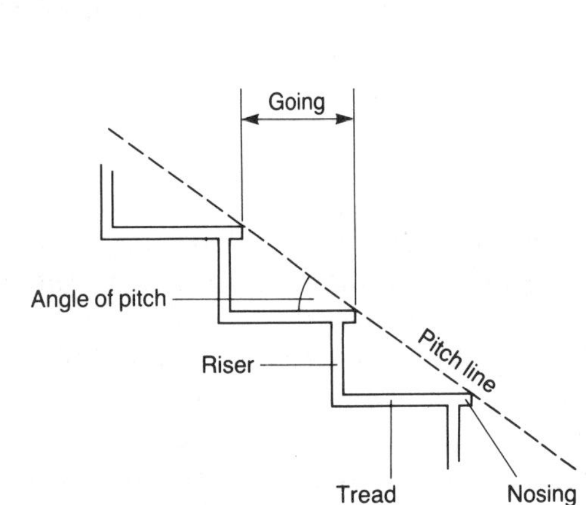

Figure 2a In a block of flats

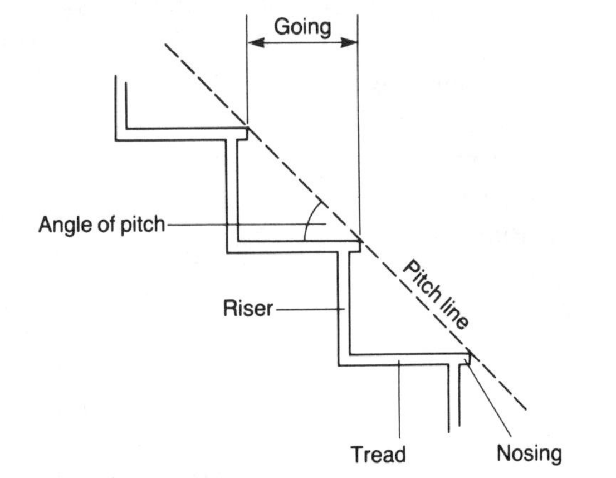

Figure 2b In a private house

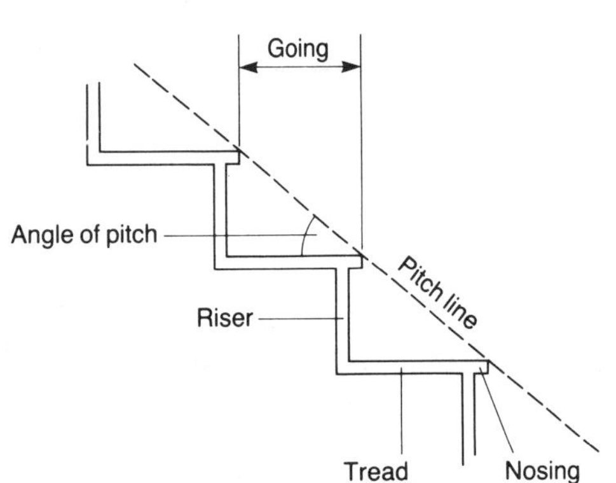

Figure 2c In a warehouse

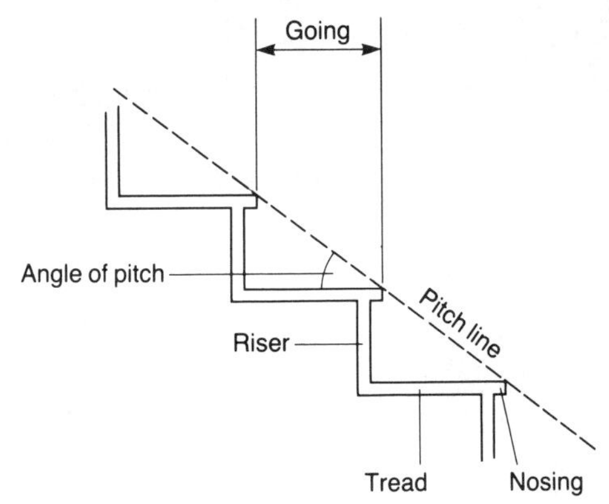

Figure 2d In a laboratory

	Location	**Angle of pitch**	**Suitable (Yes/No)**	**Reason if not suitable**
1	Office	40°	No	Too steep
2a				
2b				

Figure 3 A method of finding the angle of pitch of a staircase

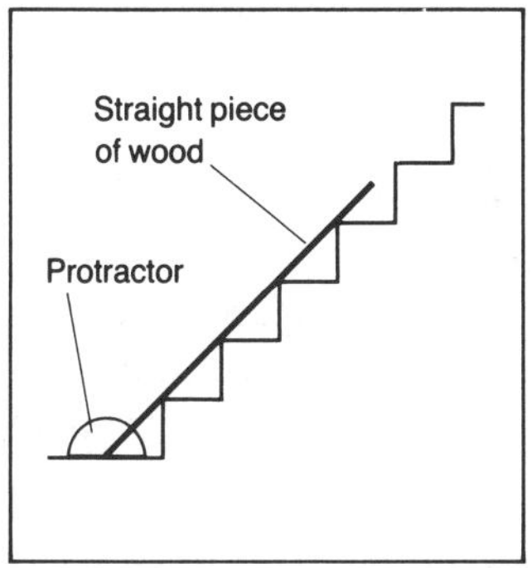

Task 2

(a) Measure the angle of pitch of staircases and steps around you and in the community, in a shopping precinct, multi-storey car park and so on. Comment on your findings. Can you find any that are too shallow? Are they really tiring to go up? A good method of measuring the pitch is shown in Figure 3.

(b) Ladders can be very dangerous if they are not put up properly. Find out (from your local DIY shop or college workshop) at what range of angles from the horizontal a ladder should be used. What will happen if the ladder is not angled properly?

Glass

The person who puts glass into windows is called a glazier. A simple calculation that a glazier has to make is to work out the area of glass in the pane. The greater the area of glass, the thicker the glass has to be, otherwise it would be unsafe. The glazier then uses a table like the one in Figure 4 to decide what thickness of glass to cut and fit.

Figure 4 Correct thicknesses of glass

Thickness (mm)	Max. area (m^2)
3	1
4	2.5
6	9

Example

A window 1.200 m wide by 2.350 m in height has area = $1.2 \times 2.35\,m^2$ = $2.82\,m^2$. This area is bigger than $2.5\,m^2$, so 4 mm glass is *unsuitable*. However, the area is less than $9\,m^2$, so 6 mm glass can be used.

Task 3

Work out the area of the following window panes. What thickness of glass should be used for each?

(a) $1.3\,m \times 0.5\,m$
(b) $1.45\,m \times 1\,m$
(c) $1.2\,m \times 1.2\,m$
(d) $2.62\,m \times 1.6\,m$
(e) $90\,cm \times 64\,cm$

Measurement for this area calculation can be to the nearest 10 mm (1 cm). But this would not be accurate enough for cutting the glass. The frame must be measured to the nearest millimetre. 5 mm is allowed for expansion of the glass in the frame, so this must be subtracted from the length and width before cutting the pane.

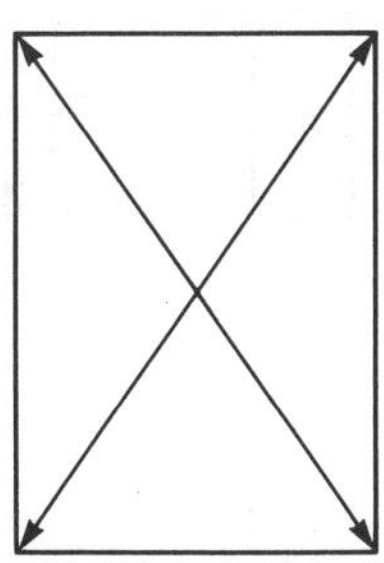

In order to check that the frame is square, the diagonal measurements should be compared. If these measurements differ then the frame cannot be a perfect rectangle, and, of course, a rectangle of glass would not fit.

This technique of checking for squareness is employed in a variety of instances in the building trade. Can you suggest some?

IMPORTANT

Read this information page
E Area and volume

13 Paperwork

AIM

To develop your skills in
- making time calculations, using the 24-hour clock
- using tables of figures to obtain data for calculations
- filling in a timesheet

Introduction

The timesheet in Figure 1 is one used by a firm of architects. You will find timesheets of one sort or another used in many types of business, not just in architect's practices. They may not be as complicated. Often a timesheet will simply be used to calculate the travelling costs and expenses for meals and refreshments that an employee can claim back.

Timesheets

At any one time, an architect may be working on a number of different jobs for different clients. The timesheet, therefore, has to be kept so that each client can be charged separately for the work done and for expenses met by the architect on each particular job.

In the example in Figure 1, the working day is considered to be 9 a.m. (09.00) to 5 p.m. (17.00), with one hour for lunch. Any work done outside of these hours would count as overtime (O/T).

Figure 1 A typical timesheet

OFFICE Ripon	NAME HR	WEEK ENDING 26-10-84	TIMESHEET

Architects, Planning, Interior Design Consultants

H.R. ARCHITECTS

Job no.	Name of Job	Date	Time		Hours		Journey to	Public Transport		Private car		Size cc		Rate	Subsistence		Total Expenses	
			from	to	day	o/t		£	p	miles	allowance £	p	parking £	p	£	p	£	p
R63	59 Laburnum Drive	22-10	09.15	12.45	3.5													
R50																		
R63							site			82								
							site			37								
Office	meeting						London	24	00	44			–	80				

Example
Architect HR starts to draw up the planning application for 59 Laburnum Drive on 22.10.84 at quarter-past nine and stops for lunch at quarter to one. This is entered on the timesheet using the 24-hour clock. The time taken, 3.5 hours, is put in the day column (because it is not overtime).

Task 1
Copy out and complete HR's timesheet.
(a) After lunch, at 2 p.m., HR continues on the work for an extension to R & M Warehouses (job no. R50). This is finished at 5 p.m.
(b) The next day HR visits the site of 59 Laburnum Drive. This takes from 11.15 in the morning until 7.30 in the evening. The round trip is 82 miles.
(c) On Wednesday 24th, HR goes to a nearby village to inspect a new milking parlour which has just been built (job no. R42). This takes her from eleven thirty to half-past five in the afternoon.
(d) On Thursday, HR continues with the warehouse extension from twenty-past nine until ten to one. In the afternoon HR finishes off the planning application for Laburnum Drive, starting at 2.15 p.m., and finishing at 4.30 p.m.
(e) On Friday, HR drives to York Railway Station (22 miles) to catch a train to London (day return £24) for a meeting. HR leaves Ripon at 7.30 in the morning and gets back home at 9 in the evening.

Travelling expenses

When someone uses their own vehicle for business reasons, they generally get an allowance per mile to cover petrol, oil, insurance and so on. This amount depends on the size of the car engine, which is measured in cc (cubic centimetres). Journeys by public transport get paid for in full.

	Engine (cc)	**Mileage allowance (p/mile)**
Motor cycle	up to 200	7.9
	201–500	8.8
	501 and over	9.4
Car	451–999	27.3
	1000–1199	30.4
	1200–1450	33.5
	1451 and over	37.0

Example
A Vauxhall Chevette has an engine size of 1256 cc. This qualifies for a mileage rate of 33.5 p. So a person who makes a journey of 26 miles in a Chevette can claim

$$26 \times 33.5\,\text{p} = 871\,\text{p} = £8.71$$

Task 2

(a) Calculate the travel claims that can be made for these journeys:
- 42 miles in a Vauxhall Cavalier (1598 cc);
- 25 miles on a Honda 125 (124 cc);
- 110 miles in a Mini 1000 (998 cc);
- 126 miles in a Renault 4 (1108 cc); and
- 55 miles on a Suzuki 550 motorcycle (572 cc).

(b) HR has a VW Golf (1043 cc). Enter the information on your copy of the timesheet. Calculate the allowance for each of the journeys shown on the timesheet.

Subsistence

When someone is working away from the office for more than just a few hours he or she may be able to claim an allowance to pay for meals and refreshments. If it is necessary to stay overnight an allowance to cover bed and breakfast is made. These are known as subsistence allowances.

Subsistence allowances	
More than 5 hours	£ 2.35
More than 10 hours	£ 5.20
Night (London)	£38.40
Night (elsewhere)	£29.15

Example
HR, who visits a site on 23 October, leaving the office at 11.15 and arriving home at 19.30, can claim a subsistence allowance of £2.35, because the absence is 8 hr. 15 min., that is, more than 5 hours but less than 10.

Task 3

(a) Calculate the other subsistence allowances that HR can claim.

(b) Work out the total expenses for each of the rows on the timesheet.

(c) What expenses will be charged to the jobs:
- R42?
- R50?
- R63?

(d) Fill in your copy of the timesheet.

IMPORTANT

Read these information pages
B Decimals
I Twenty-four-hour clock

14 In the workshop

AIM

To develop your skills in

- making approximate conversions from imperial to metric
- understanding how a simple formula is constructed, so that you can use it to solve a problem
- making decisions

Introduction

Formulae (the plural of 'formula') aren't just used by mad professors and maths teachers. Lots of people have to use formulae in their everyday work. Here are two examples in which formulae are used by engineering workers.

Using machine tools

Machinists in engineering works have to cut and shape pieces of metal using machine tools, such as lathes, drills, grinders, and milling, boring and turning machines. As you can see from the diagrams in Figure 1, either the cutter or the workpiece is rotated.

Machine tools can be set to give different cutting speeds. A typical lathe can be set to rotate at 34, 53, 68, 81, 106, 128, 162, 197, 256, 312, 394, 450, 625, 750, 900 or 1500 revolutions per minute (rpm).

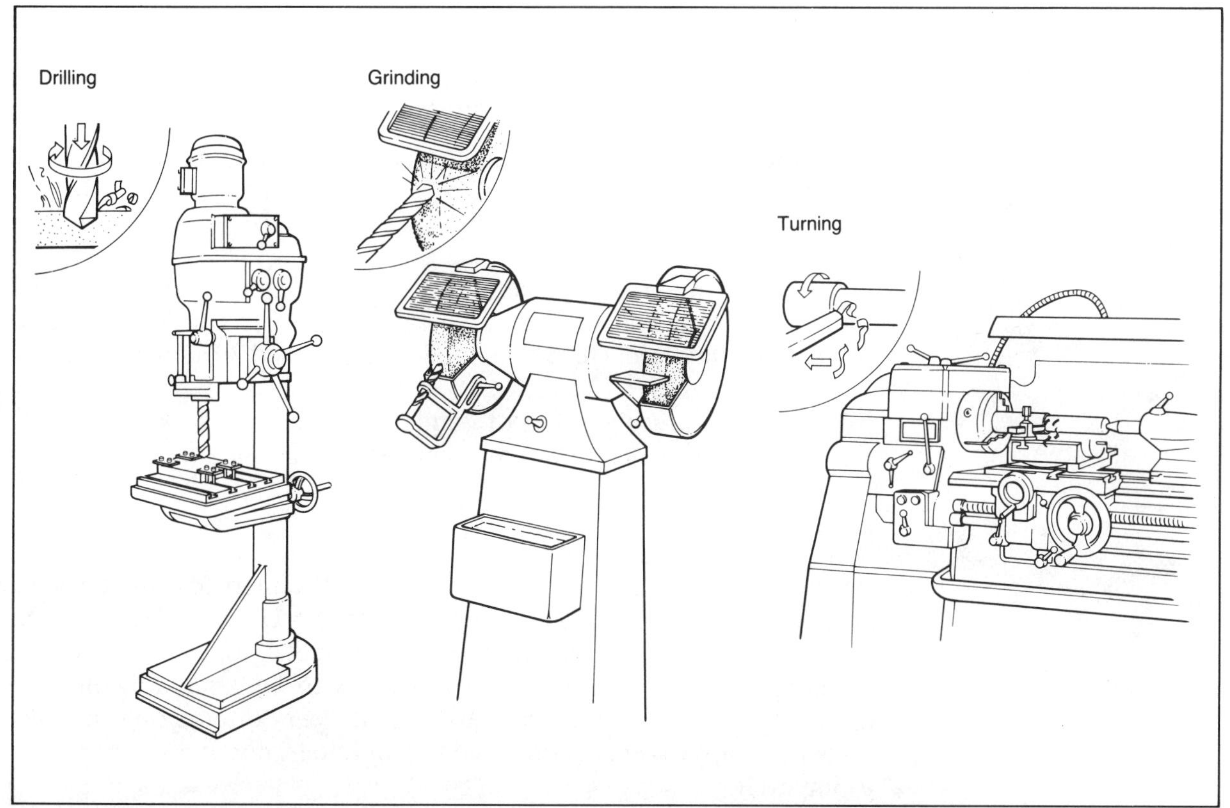

Figure 1 Some typical machine tools

Different metals need to be cut at different speeds. For instance, tough alloy steel should be cut at a speed of 30 metres/minute, while aluminium can bȩ cut at 100 metres/minute. If the speed is too high, the tool may become overheated. Time is wasted if the speed is too low, and time costs money.

A machinist has to calculate the rpm setting so that the cutting is done at the correct speed. This speed is calculated using the formula:

$$N = \frac{S}{\pi d}$$

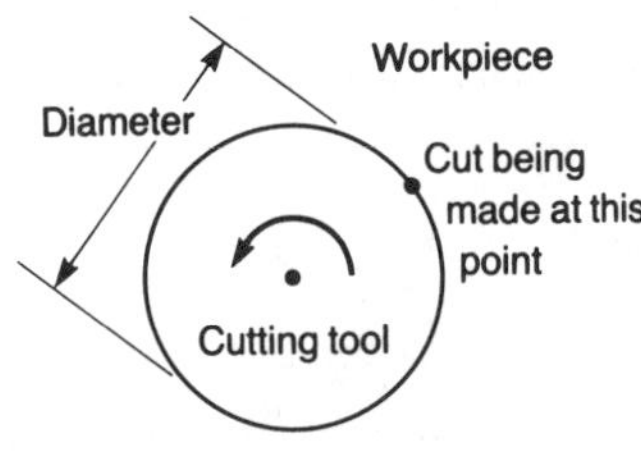

where
N is the number of rotations per minute (rpm);
S is the recommended cutting speed;
d is the diameter of the tool; and
π is a constant number: it is approximately 3.14 (it crops up whenever circles are being measured).

Example
A 14 mm drill has diameter 14 mm. That is $^{14}/_{1000} = 0.014$ m. $S =$ 30 m/min. for tough alloy steel.

$$\mathrm{N} = \frac{30}{3.14 \times 0.014}$$

$$= 682.43858 \text{ (using a calculator)}$$
$$= 682 \text{ rpm (to the nearest whole number)}$$

(625 rpm is the nearest available setting on the machine described above.)

Task 1
Using the formula, $N = S/\pi d$, calculate the recommended rpm and state the nearest available setting on a lathe for each of the following.

(a) Tough alloy steel (recommended cutting speed 30 m/min.), using a tool of diameter 12 mm.
(b) Aluminium, using a tool of diameter 8 mm.
(c) Aluminium, using a tool of diameter 25 mm.

Metrification

Because of a number of factors, including the high cost of replacing precision tools, much engineering work in the UK is still carried out using imperial measurements rather than metric ones. So a person working in the engineering industries has to be familiar with both imperial and metric units of measurement. Very often, you can make do with an approximate conversion from imperial to metric, or metric to imperial.

To convert recommended cutting speeds from imperial to metric you can use the approximation

3 ft. = 1 m

Example
For mild steel, the cutting speed = 90 ft./min.

90 ft./min. = 90 ÷ 3 m/min.
= 30 m/min.

Material	Cutting speed (ft./min.)
Mild steel	90
Medium-carbon steel	70
High-carbon steel	40
Cast iron	60
Brass	120
Aluminium	300

Task 2
Convert to metric units the cutting speeds for the materials listed in the table. Present your answers in a similar table.

Sheet-metal work

Everyone who works with sheet metal, from motor-vehicle mechanics to tinsmiths, needs to know about bending allowances.

Figure 2 A toolbox – the body

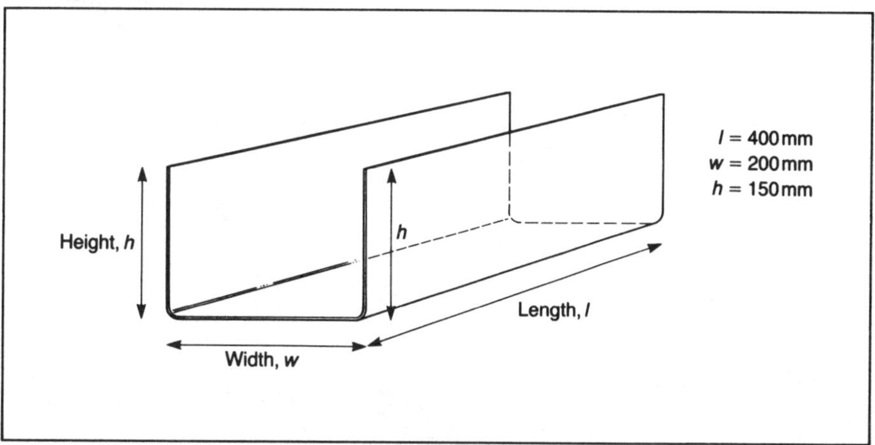

Imagine making a toolbox from sheet metal. Its body could be in the shape shown in Figure 2. Unfortunately it cannot be made simply from a piece of metal of this size:

length × (height + width + height)
= 400 mm × (150 + 200 + 150) mm
= 400 mm × 500 mm

This is because when the sheet metal is bent, the inside is compressed and the outside is stretched. The body would therefore be too big. A slightly more complicated calculation needs to be carried out to allow for this bending and stretching (see Figure 3).

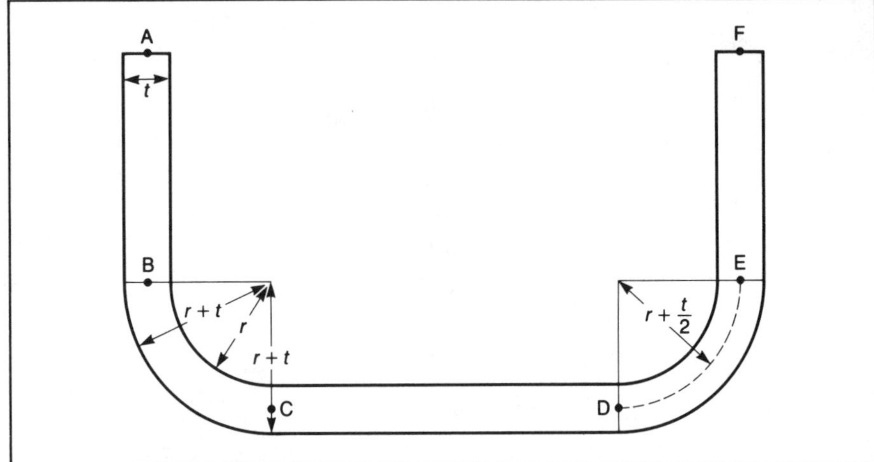

Figure 3 A toolbox – bending the body

If the thickness of metal is t, and the inside of the bend has radius r, then the outside radius will be $r + t$. However, the length of metal forming the bend has the curve shown by the dotted line, and this has radius $r + t/2$. The metal required for *each* bend = ¼ × circumference of circle with radius $r + t/2$.

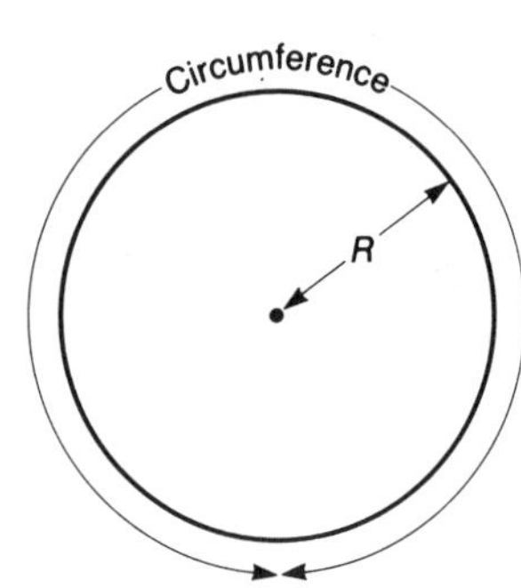

A circle with radius R has circumference $2\pi R$, so

$$BC = \tfrac{1}{4} \times 2\,\pi \left(r + \frac{t}{2}\right) = \tfrac{1}{2} \times \pi \left(r + \frac{t}{2}\right)$$

Also

$$DE = \tfrac{1}{2} \times \pi \left(r + \frac{t}{2}\right)$$

Therefore

$$BC + DE = \pi \left(r + \frac{t}{2}\right)$$

AB = required height of toolbox *minus* $(r + t)$:

$$AB = h - (r + t)$$

Similarly

$$EF = h - (r + t)$$

CD = required width of toolbox *minus* $2 \times (r + t)$:

$$CD = w - 2\,(r + t)$$

The total metal required will then be:

$$\begin{aligned} &AB + BC + CD + DE + EF \\ &= h - (r + t) + w - 2(r + t) + h - (r + t) + \pi(r + t/2) \\ &= 2h + w - 4\,(r + t) + \pi(r + t/2) \end{aligned}$$

Going back to our example, we see that we not only need to know the length, width, and height of the toolbox, but also the thickness of metal to be used and the radius of the bend.

Conversion table for material thickness

SWG*	Preferred metric (mm)
10	3.15
12	2.50
14	2.00
16	1.60
18	1.25
20	1.00
22	0.80
24	0.63

*SWG = Standard Wire Gauge

Example

20 SWG (standard wire gauge) sheet metal has a thickness of 1 mm. Suppose we have bend radius 22 mm. The piece of 20 SWG metal for the toolbox will have length 400 mm, and its other dimension will be

$$2h + w - 4(r + t) + \pi(r + t/2)$$

Now $r + t = 22 + 1 = 23$

And $r + t/2 = 22 + 0.5 = 22.5$

So $2h + w - 4(r + t) + \pi(r + t/2)$

$= 2 \times 150 + 200 - 4 \times 23 + 3.14 \times 22.5$

$= 300 + 200 - 92 + 70.65$

$= 478.65$

$= 479$ mm (to the nearest mm)

So the piece of sheet metal for the toolbox should be cut to 400 mm × 479 mm before bending.

Task 3

Calculate the size of the piece of sheet metal required for toolboxes of these dimensions. Use the conversion table for material thickness.

(a) Height 120 mm, width 170 mm, radius of bends 10 mm, length 300 mm, metal 22 SWG.

(b) Height 135 mm, width 210 mm, radius of bends 8 mm, length 350 mm, metal 24 SWG.

IMPORTANT

Read this information page
F Approximations

LIVERPOOL INSTITUTE OF HIGHER EDUCATION
THE MARKLAND LIBRARY

15 Comings and goings

AIM

To develop your skills in
- reading timetables using a 24-hour-clock
- converting from one currency to another
- constructing an appropriate travel itinerary in a given situation

Introduction
Anyone who ever travels by public transport needs to be able to read a timetable that uses the 24-hour clock. Some people need to use timetables as part of their job – bus and railway workers, for instance; also travel agents, hotel staff and secretaries.

Timetables

Task 1
You work in a hotel in Bristol. The manager of your hotel is going to a meeting in London. The taxi journey from the hotel to Bristol

Figure 1 British Rail timetable (inter-city)

Weston-super-Mare → Bristol → Swindon → London
Mondays to Fridays

				125	125	125	125	125	125	125	125	125	125	125	125	125	
		J						GP			HPQ			Q			
		2	★	①		✕ ①	①	✕ ①	①	①	✕ ①	①	①	✕ ①	①	①	⊐
Weston-super-Mare	d					06 00	—	06 25	—	07 10	—	—	07 35	—	08 05	—	—
Yatton	d					06 11	—	06 36	—	07 21	—	—	07 46	—	08 18	—	—
Nailsea & Backwell	d					06 17	—	06 42	—	07 27	—	—	07 52	—	08 26	—	—
Bristol Temple Meads	d	03 35		05 55		06 30	—	06 55	—	07 40	—	—	08 10	—	08 45	—	—
Bristol Parkway	d		05 08		06 30		06 59	—	07 29	—	07 59	—	—	08 34	—	09 04	—
Bath Spa	d	03 53		06 07		06 42	—	07 07	—	07 52	—	—	08 22	—	08 57	—	—
Chippenham	d			06 19		06 54	—	07 19	—	08 04	—	—	08 34	—	09 09	—	—
Swindon	d	04 32	05 47	06 35	07 00	07 10	07 30	07 35	08 00	08 20	08 30	08 37	08 51	09 05	—	—	09 36
Didcot	a			06 52	07 17	07 27	07 47	07 52	—	—	—	08 54	—	—	—	—	09 58
Reading E	a	05 15	06 24s	07 06	07 30	07 40	08 01	08 06	08 26	—	—	09 08	—	—	09 46	09 55	10 13
Slough	a	06 31	07 11	07 47	07 59	08 17	—	08 38	09 28	—	—	09 51	—	—	—	—	10 30
Paddington	a	06 05	07 00	07 35	08 00	08 10	08 30	08 35	08 55	09 10	09 20	09 37	09 40	09 56	10 15	10 24	10 51

Weston-super-Mare → Bristol → Swindon → London
Mondays to Fridays (continued)

		125			125	125	125	125	125	125	125	125	125	125	125	125	125
											K						
		①			✕ ①	①	①	①	①	①	⊐	✕ ①	①	①	①	①	①
Weston-super-Mare	d	—	08 53	—	09 20	—	—	11 02	11 47	—	—	—	—	13 45	—	—	14 51
Yatton	d	—	08 45	—	09 33	—	—	11 11	12 00	—	—	—	—	13 58	—	—	15 04
Nailsea & Backwell	d	—	08 51	—	09 41	—	—	—	12 08	—	—	—	—	14 06	—	—	15 12
Bristol Temple Meads	d	—	09 20	—	10 25	—	—	11 30	12 30	—	—	—	13 30	14 30	—	—	15 30
Bristol Parkway	d	09 34	—	09 47		10 43	11 37	—	—	12 43	—	13 37	—	—	14 43	15 34	—
Bath Spa	d	—	09 35	—	10 37	—	—	11 44	12 42	—	—	—	13 44	14 42	—	—	15 44
Chippenham	d	—	—	—	10 49	—	—	11 56	—	—	—	—	13 56	—	—	—	15 56
Swindon	d	—	—	10 26	11 08	11 14	12 08	12 14	13 08	13 14	13 56	14 08	14 14	15 08	15 14	—	16 13
Didcot	a	—	—	10 54	—	11 31	—	12 31	—	13 31	—	—	14 31	—	15 35	—	—
Reading E	a	10 29	10 50s	11 14	11 38	11 48	12 38	12 48	13 38	13 48	14 26	14 38	14 48	15 38	15 52	16 25	16 39
Slough	a	11 21	—	11 32	—	12 02	—	13 02	—	14 02	—	—	15 02	—	16 06	—	—
Paddington	a	10 58	11 24	11 53	12 07	12 21	13 07	13 21	14 07	14 21	14 55	15 07	15 21	16 07	16 25	16 54	17 08

Weston-super-Mare → Bristol → Swindon → London
Mondays to Fridays (continued)

		125	125	125	125	125	125	125	125	125	125	125	125	125	125	125
					FP			FO		AP						
		①	①	①	✕ ①	①	①		①	✕ ①		①	①			
Weston-super-Mare	d	—	—	—	—	—	16 20	—	17 00	—	18 15	—	—	20 00	20 40	—
Yatton	d	—	—	—	—	—	16 33	—	17 13	●	18 28	—	—	20 11	—	—
Nailsea & Backwell	d	—	—	—	—	—	16 41	—	17 21	—	18 36	—	—	20 17	—	—
Bristol Temple Meads	d	—	16 00	—	16 40	—	17 10	17 35	17 55	—	18 55	—	—	20 30	21 20	—
Bristol Parkway	d	15 50	—	16 19	—	17 14	—	—	—	18 14	—	19 14	20 09	—	—	21 59
Bath Spa	d	—	16 14	—	16 54	—	17 22	17 47	18 07	—	19 07	—	—	20 42	21 32	—
Chippenham	d	—	16 26	—	17 06	—	17 34	—	18 19	—	19 19	—	—	20 54	21 44	—
Swindon	d	16 21	16 41	16 50	17 25	—	17 51	18 12	18 36	18 45	19 36	19 45	20 41	21 12	22 01	22 30
Didcot	a	16 38	—	—	17 40	—	18 08	—	18 53	—	—	20 02	—	21 29	22 18	—
Reading E	a	16 52	17 09	17 18	17 53	18 05	18 21	—	19 06	19 12	20 02	20 15	21 06	21 42	22 31	22 56
Slough	a	17 08	—	18 01	18 07	—	1902	—	—	19 26	—	20 29	21 43	21 57	—	23 39
Paddington	a	17 26	17 38	17 47	18 26	18 34	18 51	19 00	19 35	19 45	20 32	20 48	21 35	22 16	23 01	23 25

Bristol — Avonmouth and Severn Beach
Second Class only unless otherwise shown **Mondays to Saturdays**

Miles		BHX		BHX A		BHX		A						SX		SO		SX		SO						A FO
0	Severn Beach d	0558	....	....	....	0650	....	....	....	0756	....	0858	....	0953	....	0958	....	1046	....	1050	....	1217	....	1357	....	....
3¼	St.Andrew's Road d	0606	..	..	..	0658	..	..	..	0804	..	0906	..	1001	..	1006	..	1054	..	1058	..	1225	..	1405	..	..
4½	Avonmouth d	0609	....	....	....	0701	....	....	....	0807	....	0909	....	1004	....	1009	....	1057	....	1101	....	1228	....	1408	....	....
6	Shirehampton d	0613	..	..	..	0705	..	..	..	0811	..	0913	..	1008	..	1013	..	1101	..	1105	..	1232	..	1412	..	..
7¼	Sea Mills d	0617	....	....	....	0709	....	....	....	0815	....	0917	....	1012	....	1017	....	1105	....	1109	....	1236	....	1416	....	....
9¼	Clifton Down d	0623	..	..	..	0715	..	..	..	0823	..	0923	..	1018	..	1023	..	1111	..	1115	..	1242	..	1422	..	..
10½	Redland d	0625	....	....	....	0717	....	....	....	0825	....	0925	....	1020	....	1025	....	1113	....	1117	....	1244	....	1424	....	....
10¾	Montpelier d	0627	..	..	..	0719	..	..	..	0827	..	0927	..	1022	..	1027	..	1115	..	1119	..	1246	..	1426	..	..
12	Stapleton Road d	0631	....	0654	....	0723	....	0734	....	0831	....	0931	....	1026	....	1031	....	1119	....	1123	....	1250	....	1430	....	1556
12¼	Lawrence Hill d	0634	..	..	..	0726	..	0737	..	0834	..	0934	..	1029	..	1034	..	1122	..	1126	..	1253	..	1433	..	1559
13½	Bristol Temple Meads a	0638	....	0701	....	0730	....	0742	....	0838	....	0938	....	1033	....	1038	....	1125	....	1130	....	1257	....	1437	....	1602

		SO		SX		A MFSX		A MO		BHX				A		BHX										
Severn Beach d		1540	....	1545	....	....	....	....	....	1645	....	1726	....	....	....	1830	....	1900	....	2033	....	2212	....	....	....	....
St.Andrew's Road d		1548	..	1553	..	..	..	..	..	1701b	..	1734	..	..	..	1838	..	1908	..	2041	..	2220	..	..	..	..
Avonmouth d		1551	....	1556	....	....	....	....	....	1704	....	1737	....	....	....	1841	....	1911	....	2044	....	2223	....	....	....	....
Shirehampton d		1555	..	1600	..	..	..	..	..	1708	..	1741	..	..	..	1845	..	1915	..	2048	..	2227	..	..	..	..
Sea Mills d		1559	....	1604	....	....	....	....	....	1712	....	1745	....	....	....	1849	....	1919	....	2052	....	2231	....	....	....	....
Clifton Down d		1605	..	1610	..	..	..	..	..	1718	..	1752	..	..	..	1855	..	1925	..	2058	..	2237	..	..	..	..
Redland d		1607	....	1612	....	....	....	....	....	1720	....	1754	....	....	....	1857	....	1927	....	2100	....	2239	....	....	....	....
Montpelier d		1609	..	1614	..	..	..	..	..	1722	..	1756	..	..	..	1859	..	1929	..	2102	..	2241	..	..	..	..
Stapleton Road d		1613	....	1618	....	1622	....	1652	....	1727	....	1802	....	1901	....	1904	....	1933	....	2106	....	2245	....	....	....	....
Lawrence Hill d		1616	..	1621	..	1625	..	1655	..	1730	..	1805	..	..	..	1907	..	1936	..	2109	..	2248	..	..	..	..
Bristol Temple Meads a		1620	....	1625	....	1628	....	1658	....	1733	....	1808	....	1906	....	1910	....	1940	....	2113	....	2252	....	....	....	....

A First and Second Class   b Arr. 1653

Figure 2 British Rail timetable (local)

Parkway station takes 40 minutes, and the journey from Paddington to the meeting takes 30 minutes. You have to book her taxi. At what time should she leave the hotel if she is to reach the meeting at:

(a) 10.30 a.m.?
(b) 11.00 a.m.?
(c) 2.15 p.m.?
(d) 3.00 p.m.?
(e) 4.00 p.m.?

In all cases, state the arrival and departure times of the trains she could catch.

Task 2

Your hotel is close to Sea Mills Station, which is served by the British Rail Avonlink Service (Figure 2). Some guests wish to leave for London as soon as possible. They plan to catch the Avonlink train to Temple Meads and then a train to Paddington. What trains would you suggest they catch if it is now:

(a) 11.00 a.m. on a Friday?
(b) 9.00 a.m.?
(c) 8.00 a.m.?

Cashing traveller's cheques

A hotel receptionist normally has a wide range of responsibilities. These may include cashing traveller's cheques for foreign visitors. This has to be done very carefully, making sure that the correct rate of exchange is used. The rate of exchange can be obtained by telephone from the hotel's bank or by looking in one of the main daily newspapers.

Example
£1 = \$1.2240, so $£\frac{1}{1.2240} = \$1$.

150 dollars of US traveller's cheques is equivalent to

$$150 \times \frac{1}{1.2240}$$
$$= 150 \div 1.2240$$
$$= £122.55 \text{ (to the nearest penny)}$$

Task 3
Using the exchange rates in Figure 3, calculate the equivalent amount of sterling (£p) for these traveller's cheques:
(a) \$100 (United States)
(b) \$200 (Canada)
(c) 500 Fr (France)
(d) 400 Swiss Francs
(e) 1000 DM (W. Germany)

Figure 3 Exchange rates

Tourist Exchange Rates
We buy Traveller's Cheques at:

Austria	26.250	Italy	2307.25
Belgium	75.000	Portugal	200.75
Canada	1.6100	Spain	208.50
Rep. of Ireland	1.2025	Sweden	10.5625
France	11.3925	Switzerland	3.0450
W. Germany	3.7125	USA	1.2240
Greece	153.00		

IMPORTANT

Read these information pages
F Approximations
I Twenty-four-hour clock

LIVERPOOL INSTITUTE OF
HIGHER EDUCATION
THE MARKLAND LIBRARY

16 On sale

AIM

To develop your skills in
- increasing and decreasing prices by a given percentage
- using mark-up, VAT and discount in retail applications

Introduction

These were some of the ways people did their sums before everyone had electronic calculators:
- in their heads (still useful once in a while!);
- with a mechanical calculator (noisy and quite hard work);
- on paper using a pencil (quiet, but hard work);
- with a slide rule (nicknamed the 'guessing stick');
- by looking in a ready reckoner (a book of tables); and
- with an abacus (especially if they were Chinese or Japanese).

A shop manager might well have used a calculator like the one shown in the photograph. It helps work out mark-up and profit margin, and could even work out VAT (value-added tax).

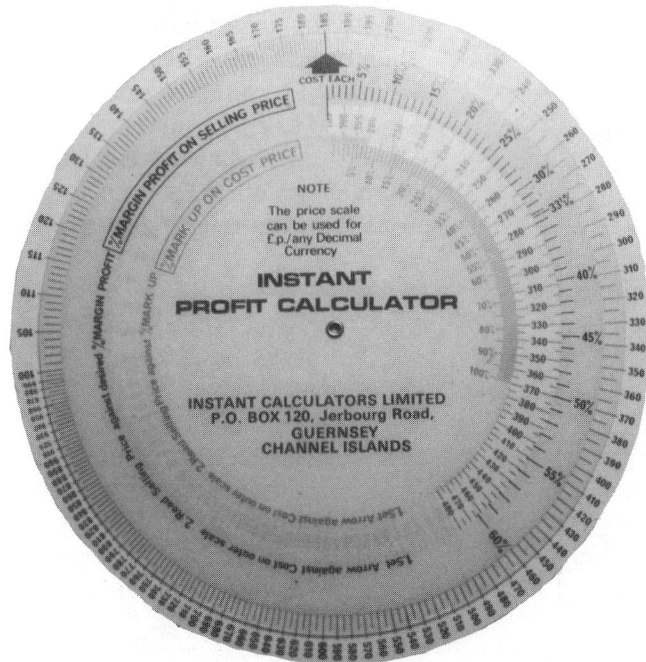

Mark-up

Shops often work out the price at which they are going to sell an article by increasing the cost price (the price they paid for it) by a certain percentage. This is known as the mark-up. Books, for instance, have a mark-up of 50 per cent.

Example

The cost price of a book is £2.50.
It will sell in a shop for £2.50 plus 50% of £2.50.
50% of £2.50 is the same as ½ of £2.50, which is £1.25.
So the selling price = £2.50 + £1.25 = £3.75.

Task 1

Work out the selling price in each of these examples.

	Cost price	Mark-up
(a)	68p	50%
(b)	45p	20%
(c)	£1.60	30%
(d)	£1.00	35%
(e)	£2.43	33⅓%

H SAMUEL
AT DEBENHAMS
OXFORD STREET

02/04/85 13:50 HM 01 8986

SALE

09 V129 CLOCK 7.95
TOTAL 7.95
CASH 10.00
CHANGE 2.05

VAT NO: 109 3531 86

BRITAIN'S LARGEST JEWELLER

	CODE	GOODS	VAT RATE
	1	19·40	
	2	16·10	
Sub Total		35-50	
VAT @ 15%		5-33	
TOTAL £		40-83.	
Less Deposit £		20-00	
BALANCE DUE £		20-83.	

Value-added tax (VAT)

Value-added tax is what is known as an indirect tax. This is because it taxes people on what they buy instead of what they earn. If you don't buy anything, you don't pay any of this sort of tax! Food and some other basic necessities are not taxed, but almost everything else is. VAT applies to services as well. This means that food from a takeaway is taxed because a service has been done in cooking it.

The standard rate of VAT in 1985 was 15 per cent. Most shops now simply include VAT in the price they show on the ticket. Some add it on as a separate item on the bill.

Example

A pair of windscreen wipers cost £3.04 plus VAT at 15 per cent.
VAT will be 15% of £3.04.
1% of £3.04 = 3.04p.
So
VAT = 15% of £3.04
= 15 × 3.04p
= 45.6p
= 46p (to the nearest penny)
So the price including VAT = £3.04 + £0.46 = £3.50.

Task 2

How much will these prices increase when VAT is added?

(a) 80p
(b) £4.00
(c) £2.50
(d) £1.29
(e) £13.65

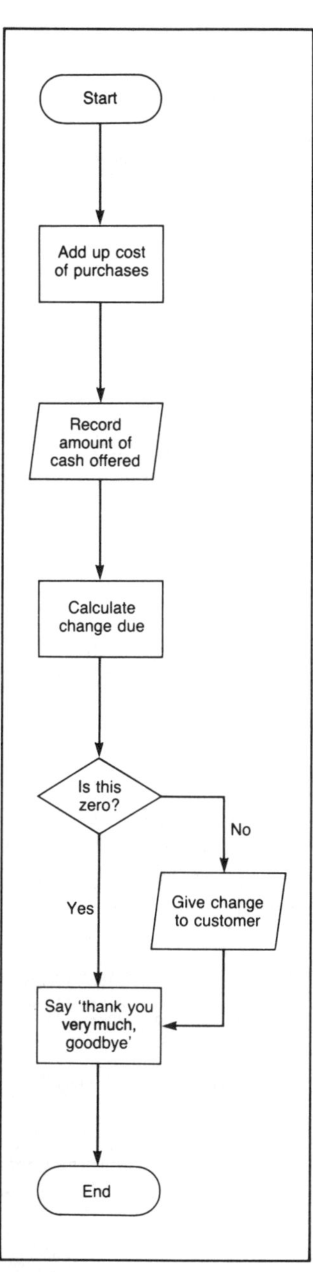

Figure 1 Flow chart for a cash purchase

Discounts

The most common way of giving a discount is to take a percentage off the price.

Example

A builder's merchant offers 10 per cent discount to account holders.

A sink unit costs £95.75.
The discount will be 10% of £95.75.
1% of £95.75 = 95.75p.
Discount = 10% of £95.75
= 10 × 95.75p
= 957.5p
= £9.58 (to the nearest penny)
The discounted price is therefore £95.75 − £9.58 = £86.17.

Task 3

(a) What is the price of these items after discount?

Item	Price	Discount	Discounted price
Wheelbarrow	£21	10%	
Timber	£35.50	10%	
Tyre	£19.60	5%	
Hire equipment	£73.26	20%	
Paint	£14.53	5%	

(b) VAT should be added to the cost of the sink unit in the example above. Work out the price including VAT of 15 per cent

- if VAT is added to £95.75 and then the discount is given; and
- if VAT is added to the discounted price of £86.17.

What do you notice?

Task 4

This flow chart in Figure 1 shows the process a shop assistant might go through when a customer buys things for cash. Draw a flow chart to show the process the assistant would go through if the customer paid by cheque (with a cheque guarantee card). Make sure that you check the cheque for errors and that the signature is the same as on the guarantee card.

IMPORTANT

Read this information page
D Percentages

17 Solid foundations

AIM

To develop your skills in
- multiplying simple fractions by whole numbers
- determining volume from given dimensions
- using numbers in situations found in the building trade

Introduction

Concrete is made from a mixture of cement, sand, aggregate (small stones) and water. Mixing concrete requires some knowledge of ratios, as different mixtures are needed for different purposes. Foundations, for instance, require a mix of one part of cement to three parts of sand to six parts of aggregate. This is expressed as a mix of 1 : 3 : 6 (said 'one to three to six'). Water is added to produce a dense mixture which must not be too wet or too dry – a wet mixture produces a weak concrete, a dry mix is difficult to work.

Mixing concrete

It is best to base a mix of concrete on one complete bag of cement. This is because cement loses strength if kept too long and especially if in an opened bag.

Nowadays you buy cement in 50 kg bags. These are very slightly smaller than the 1 cwt (hundredweight) bags which were available in pre-metrification days in the UK. Many builders still prefer to use imperial measurements and they treat the 50 kg bags as though they were 1 cwt. The other two ingredients of concrete, sand and aggregate, are sold by volume.

A gauge box (Figure 1) is often used to measure them out. This is a deep and narrow box which should either hold the full amount for a batch of concrete, or an exact fraction. A gauge box 12 in. × 12 in. × 18 in. deep will hold $1 \times 1 \times 1\frac{1}{2}$ cu. ft. = $1\frac{1}{2}$ cu. ft. (12 in. = 1 ft.). A recommended metric box has dimensions 350 mm × 350 mm × 410 mm.

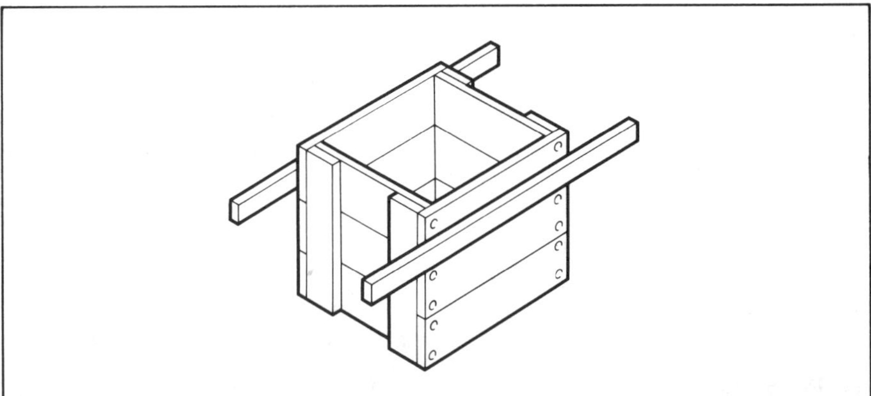

Figure 1 A gauge box

Task 1

(a) What volume would a recommended metric gauge box contain? Before you do the multiplication, convert the measurements to metres and give your answer in cubic metres (m^3).

(b) Can you suggest dimensions for a metric gauge box with volume $0.035\,m^3$?

The table in Figure 2 shows different mixtures for concrete together with some uses.

Figure 2 Mixes of concrete

Mix	Cement	Sand	Aggregate	Use
1:3:6	50 kg .... 1 cwt.	.... $3\frac{3}{4}$ cu. ft.	.... $7\frac{1}{2}$ cu. ft.	Foundations; solid ground floor
1:2:4	50 kg .... 1 cwt.	....	....	General purposes; walls
$1:1\frac{1}{2}:3$	50 kg .... 1 cwt.	....	....	Watertight and strong concrete

Note: 50 kg of cement has volume $0.035\,m^3$ (approx). 1 cwt. has volume $1\frac{1}{4}$ cu. ft. (approximately).

Example

Mixture for a solid ground floor, using 1 cwt. of cement:

	1	: **3**	: **6**	
by volume:	$1 \times 1\frac{1}{4}$	$3 \times 1\frac{1}{4}$	$6 \times 1\frac{1}{4}$	cu. ft.
	$= 1\frac{1}{4}$	$= 3\frac{3}{4}$	$= 6\frac{6}{4} = 7\frac{2}{4} = 7\frac{1}{2}$	
	cement	sand	aggregate	

Task 2

(a) What volumes of sand and aggregate should go in the spaces in the table in Figure 2? Copy and complete the table.

(b) What do you think would be the most suitable dimensions for an imperial gauge box? (Imperial measurements are feet, inches, hundredweight, etc.)

Price guides for builders

A builder is generally expected to quote a price before being contracted to carry out a job. To help a builder do this, price guides are regularly published which take account of current prices and wage

rates. One such is the *Hutchins' Priced Schedule* which is published annually. This is advertised with the slogan, 'Profits Depend on Estimating'. In order to use it, a builder simply has to measure up the job and then carry out a simple calculation.

Example
For a concrete floor, concrete – 1 : 2 : 6, 150 mm thick, spread over the site and levelled – is priced in the 1984 guide at £59.92 per cubic metre. This includes the labour costs of 7.00 man-hours.

A floor measuring 2.4 m by 4.4 m (the kitchen of 59 Laburnum Drive on page 54) has area $2.4 \times 4.4 = 10.56\,\text{m}^2$.

The volume of concrete will be $10.56 \times 0.150 = 1.584\,\text{m}^3$. (150 mm = 0.150 m.)

The cost will be 1.584 × £59.92 = £94.91328.

This job should be quoted at £94.91 (to the nearest penny).

And it will take $1.584 \times 7.00 = 11.088$ man-hours. This last figure will help the builder work out a time schedule.

Task 3

(a) Calculate the prices for these concrete floors:
- 3.1 m × 4.2 m, 150 mm thick; and
- 2.9 m × 3.7 m, 150 mm thick.

(b) Plastering is priced per square metre. In the 1984 guide, two coats of Carlite plaster to brickwork is quoted at £4.02. Calculate the prices for plastering these walls with Carlite plaster:
- 4.4 m × 2.4 m (the living room at 59 Laburnum Drive); and
- 5.6 m × 2.2 m.

(c) Plumbing in 15 mm copper pipework is priced at £2.78 per linear metre. How much should these jobs be quoted at?
- 15 m
- 126 m

IMPORTANT

Read these information pages
B Decimals
C Fractions
E Area and volume

The photograph shows a device used by plumbers to put bends in pipework. It can be used to bend copper and steel light-gauge tube for water and gas services.

18 At the office

AIM

To develop your skills in

- calculating the whole from percentages
- using numbers in money and time applications
- filling in forms
- using international time zones in business situations

Introduction

Clock time varies from country to country around the world. It is worked out so that the sun is highest in the sky at approximately 12 noon (midday). In some large countries there are time bands across the country. In the USA, for instance, there are a number of different time zones, and the time in New York on the East coast is three hours different from the time in San Francisco on the West coast.

It would obviously be pointless for a business in Britain to telephone a firm in Australia in the middle of the night! Being able to work out time differences between different countries is a skill an office receptionist is expected to have. The rest of us need to know for other reasons – a friend in Australia wouldn't like to be woken at 4 a.m., even if it was to wish him 'happy birthday'.

International time

Figure 1 is a map of the world showing the time differences based on Greenwich Mean Time (GMT), the time in Britain. (GMT is the time in Britain only during the winter months. During the summer we use

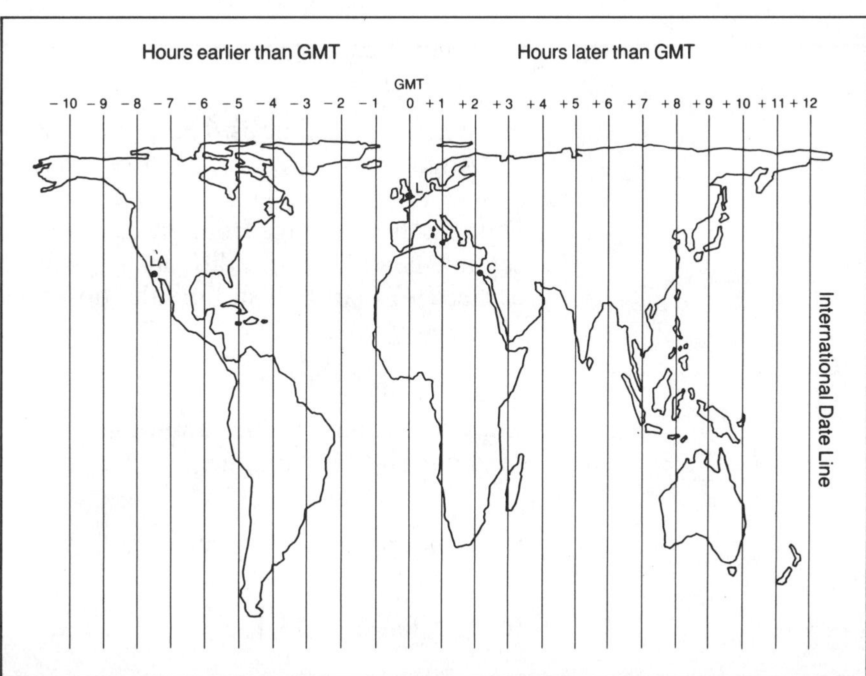

Figure 1 World map, showing approximate time differences from GMT. LA = Los Angeles, L = London, C = Cairo (based on the Peters Projection)

BST or British Summer Time, which is one hour later than GMT.) The map is only approximate: more accurate time differences can be found in the booklet of *Telephone Dialling Codes*.

Examples

(a) Los Angeles is 8 hours earlier (−8) than GMT.
- So when London time is 9 a.m., it is 8 hours earlier in Los Angeles → 1 a.m. in Los Angeles.
- And when Los Angeles time is 2 p.m., it is 8 hours later in London → 10 p.m. in London.

(b) Cairo is 2 hours later (+2) than GMT.
- So when London time is 10.45 a.m., it is 2 hours later in Cairo → 12.45 p.m. in Cairo.
- And when Cairo time is 13.35, it is 2 hours earlier in London → 11.35 in London.

Task 1

Copy and complete the following:

(a) When London time is 10.45 a.m., it is . . . hours earlier/later in Los Angeles → . . . . in Los Angeles.

(b) When London time is 11.37, it is . . . hours earlier/later in Cairo, → . . . . in Cairo.

(c) When Cairo time is 15.20, it is . . . hours earlier/later in London → . . . . in London.

(d) When Los Angeles time is 10 p.m., it is . . . hours earlier/later in London → . . . . in London.

(e) When Cairo time is 6.30 p.m., it is . . . hours earlier/later in Los Angeles → . . . . in Los Angeles.

Figure 2 shows a page from the *Telephone Dialling Codes* booklet. The column headed 'Time diff. in hrs' tells you how much later (+) or earlier (−) than British time the different countries are.

Task 2

Copy and complete the following:

(a) London time 10 a.m. → 5½ hrs later → Sri Lanka time
→ ....

(b) London time 4.30 p.m. → .... → Tanzania time
→ ....

(c) London time 14.15 → .... → Trinidad time
→ ....

Figure 2 Part of the *Telephone Dialling Codes* booklet

Country		IDD Code	Operator services dial	Dir. enqs. dial	Time diff. in hrs.	Charge Band (IDD)	(Op.)
Sierra Leone		**010 232•**	155	155	0	5A	5
Singapore		**010 65•**	155	155	+7	5B	5
Solomon Islands			155	155	+11		5
Somali Democratic Republic			155	155	+3		5
South Africa		**010 27†**	155	155	+2	5A	5
Bloemfontein	**51**	*East London*	**431**	*Port Elizabeth*			**41**
Cape Town	**21**	*Johannesburg*	**11**	*Pretoria*			**12**
Durban	**31**						
South West Africa — See Namibia							
Spain		**010 34†**	155	155	+1	2	2
Alicante	**65**	*Ibiza*	**71**	*Santa Cruz (Tenerife)*			**22**
Barcelona	**3**	*Las Palmas*	**28**	*Santander*			**42**
Benidorm	**65**	*Madrid*	**1**	*Seville*			**54**
Bilbao	**4**	*Malaga*	**52**	*Torremolinos*			**52**
Granada	**58**	*Palma (Majorca)*	**71**	*Valencia*			**6**
Sri Lanka		**010 94†**	155	155	+5½	5B	5
Colombo Central	**1**	*Kandy*	**8**	*Katunayake Int. Airport*			**315**
Sudan (Dem. Rep. of)			155	155	+2		5
Surinam (Republic of)			155	155	−3½		5
Swaziland		**010 268•**	155	155	+2	5A	5
Sweden		**010 46†**	155	155	+1	2	2
Gothenburg	**31**	*Malmo*	**40**	*Stockholm*			**8**
Helsingborg	**42**	*Norrkoping*	**11**	*Uppsala*			**18**
Linkoping	**13**	*Orebro*	**19**	*Vasteras*			**21**
Switzerland		**010 41†**	155	155	+1	2	2
Basle	**61**	*Lausanne*	**21**	*St. Moritz*			**82**
Berne	**31**	*Lucerne*	**41**	*Winterthur*			**52**
Geneva	**22**	*St. Gallen*	**71**	*Zurich*			**1**
Interlaken	**36**						
Syrian Arab Republic			155	155	+2		5
Taiwan		**010 886†**	155	155	+8	5B	5
Kaohsiung	**7**	*Taipei*	**2**				
Tanzania		**010 255†**	155	155	+3	5A	5
Dar es Salaam	**51**						
Thailand		**010 66†**	155	155	+7	5B	5
Bangkok	**2**	*Thonburi*	**2**				
Togo			155	155	0		5
Tonga		**010 676•**	155	155	+13	5B	5
Trinidad and Tobago		**010 1 809•**	155	155	−4	4	4
Tristan Da Cunha			155	155	0		5
Tunisia		**010 216†**	155	155	+1	3	3
Sousse	**3**	*Tunis*	**1**				
Turkey		**010 90†**	155	155	+3	3	3
Ankara	**41**	*Istanbul*	**11**	*Izmir*			**51**
Turks and Caicos Islands		**010 1 809 946•**	155	155	−5	4	4

•No Area Code required.
†If the code for the town you require is not listed ask the international operator for it. Many more Area Codes are shown in the International Telephone Guide, available free by dialling 100 and asking for Freefone 2013 (during normal working hours).

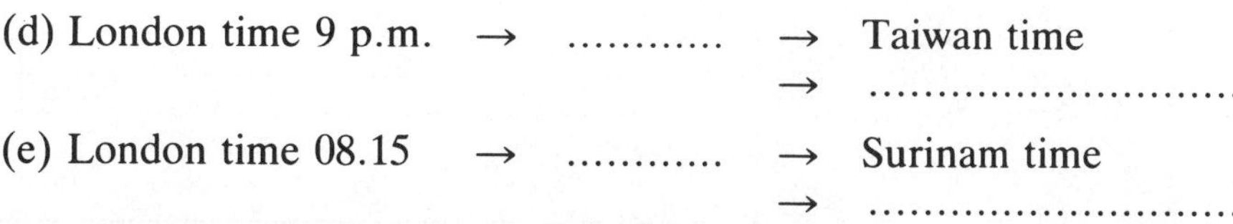

(d) London time 9 p.m. → .... → Taiwan time → ....

(e) London time 08.15 → .... → Surinam time → ....

Petty cash

In almost every firm a great number of cash payments are made. These include payments for items the office has run out of and needs urgently (such as pencils, for example). The money for these payments is generally taken out of what is known as the 'petty cash'. The petty cash must, of course, be accounted for, penny by penny, and recorded in the Petty Cash Book.

Before this, however, the person making each payment will probably be required to fill in a voucher detailing the purchase made. A typical petty-cash voucher is shown here:

petty cash claim

name: date:

required for	VAT Amount		Amount incl. VAT	
Total:				

signed: passed: folio:

Often it is very easy to complete a voucher like this, because the shop from which the purchase is made will show the price excluding VAT and the VAT amount separately. Simple addition will give the amount including VAT.

Example

Envelopes costing £1.26 + 19p VAT would be entered on the voucher like this:

petty cash claim

name: date:

required for	VAT Amount		Amount incl. VAT	
Envelopes		19	1	45
Total:				

signed: passed: folio:

Task 3

Copy the petty-cash voucher and enter the following items:
(a) Envelopes costing £1.26 + 19p VAT;
(b) Correcting fluid costing 68p + 10p VAT; and
(c) A packet of document wallets costing £7.56 + £1.13 VAT.
Total the amounts in the space provided, date and sign the voucher.

Sometimes the purchaser has to calculate how much of the total purchase price is VAT. This cannot be done simply by finding 15 per cent of the purchase price. In the envelopes example, for instance:

15% of £1.45 = 21.75p, *not* 19p

It has to be thought out like this:

If the *excluding VAT* price is 100%, then the *including VAT* price is 115% of the *excluding VAT* price.

So 115% of the excluding VAT price = 145p

1% of the excluding VAT price $= \frac{145}{115}$

= 1.2608696p

15% of the excluding VAT price $= 15 \times \frac{145}{115}$

= 18.913043p

and this is the VAT amount.

So we can say the VAT amounts to 19p (to the nearest penny).

IMPORTANT

Read these information pages
A Place value
D Percentages
I Twenty-four-hour clock

Task 4

Copy the petty-cash voucher again and enter the following items. You will need to calculate the VAT amount in each case.
(a) Adler electronic typewriter ribbon, £3.75.
(b) Sheet of Letraset, £4.37.
(c) Jar of coffee, £1.37 (there is no VAT on coffee).
(d) Airmail padded envelope, 30p.
Complete the voucher.

LIVERPOOL INSTITUTE OF HIGHER EDUCATION
THE MARKLAND LIBRARY

19 On the shelf

AIM

To develop your skills in
- determining the size of number using place value
- classifying books according to a number system
- manipulating numbers to generate or check a test digit

Introduction

Books are not just flung randomly onto library shelves. If they were, people would spend ages looking for the book they wanted.

The books are put into some kind of order. Fiction is always arranged alphabetically according to the author's surname. Non-fiction, however, is generally organised into topics. This is so that a reader can see all the books available on a particular topic together on the shelves. In most public libraries the system used for sorting or classifying non-fiction books is the Dewey Decimal System.

The Dewey Decimal System

Without going into too much detail, the basic system is this. Each topic is given a decimal number. All books on exactly the same subject have the same classification number. They will appear together on the shelves. If there is a slight difference in what two books cover, then there will be a small difference in their Dewey numbers, and they will be near each other on the shelves.

One of the non-fiction catalogues of index cards will be arranged in this order as well.

Figure 1 shows a list of books found on part of an 'oversize books' shelf. The books are arranged from left to right according to the Dewey code. You can see how the decimal number increases. A book entitled *Industrial Pollution*, with Dewey number 628.5, would go where shown by the arrow (←).

Figure 1 Examples of Dewey numbers

Earthquake Engineering	624.176	
Structural Engineering Design in Practice	624.1771	
Design of Loadbearing Brickwork	624.1836	
Concrete Bridge Designer's Manual	624.25	
Handbook of Highway Engineering	625.7	
Practical Hydraulics	627	
Waste Disposal Management and Practice	628.445	
		←
Aviation/Space Dictionary	629.1303	
Ballooning	629.13322	
Aircraft Gas-Turbine Engine Technology	629.13435	
International Airport	629.136	
The Airport	629.136	
Car Maintenance Made Easy	629.2	

Task 1

Where would these oversize books be placed on the shelf?

(a) *Airships for the Future*	629.13324
(b) *Steel Box-Girder Bridges*	624.4
(c) *The Engineering of Large Dams*	627.8
(d) *Concorde*	629.133
(e) *Water and Waste Water Technology*	628.1

Computers in the book trade

Nowadays more and more computers are being used in the world of books. Publishers, bookshops and libraries are becoming computerised. This is because computers are able to process masses and masses of information in a very short time.

Every single book title is given a number by its publisher. So instead of referring to a book by its title, author and so on, all that is necessary to identify a book is to give its number – its ISBN (International Standard Book Number).

The ISBN is a string of ten digits which indicate the language, the publisher and the title of the book.

Example
Homage to Catalonia by George Orwell, published by Penguin in 1962

The final 6 is the check digit. It is calculated from the other digits like this. The first digit is multiplied by ten; the second by nine; and so on. These answers are then added together.

$0 \times 10 = 0$
$1 \times 9 = 9$
$4 \times 8 = 32$
$0 \times 7 = 0$
$0 \times 6 = 0$
$1 \times 5 = 5$
$6 \times 4 = 24$
$9 \times 3 = 27$
$9 \times 2 = 18$
115

The total is divided by 11: 115 ÷ 11 = 10 remainder 5. The remainder is subtracted from 11: 11 − 5 = 6. This gives the check digit.

A small error made when ordering a book by giving its title, author, publisher and so on, such as

Homage to Catalonia, George Orwill, Penguin, 1962

would not create any problems. However, mistakes are often made with long strings of numbers: unless a check is incorporated, this could easily go unnoticed. Our example ISBN might for example be given as 0 14 001969 6 and this will refer to a completely different book. The error may slip through unless the check is made:

$0 \times 10 = 0$	Check
$1 \times 9 = 9$	Total divided by 11:
$4 \times 8 = 32$	118 ÷ 11 = 10 remainder 8
$0 \times 7 = 0$	
$0 \times 6 = 0$	Remainder subtracted from 11:
$1 \times 5 = 5$	11 − 8 = 3
$9 \times 4 = 36$	
$6 \times 3 = 18$	This does *not* agree with the check digit,
$9 \times 2 = 18$	so a mistake has been made.
Total 118	

Example
What should the check digit be for *The Alien Sky* by Paul Scott, published by Granada in 1974? The ISBN is 0 586 03871 ■.

$0 \times 10 = 0$	Total divided by 11:
$5 \times 9 = 45$	$221 \div 11 = 20$ remainder 1
$8 \times 8 = 64$	
$6 \times 7 = 42$	Remainder subtracted from 11:
$0 \times 6 = 0$	$11 - 1 = 10$
$3 \times 5 = 15$	
$8 \times 4 = 32$	Check digit should be 10,
$7 \times 3 = 21$	but this is not a single digit
$1 \times 2 = 2$	so X is used instead.
Total 221	

The ISBN in full is 0 586 03871 X.

Task 2

(a) What should the check digits be for these ISBNs:
- 0 86318 025 ■ (*Yan Kit's Classic Chinese Cookbook* by Yan Kit So)?
- 2 264 00932 ■ (*L'Ecume Des Jours* by Boris Vian)?
- 0 436 45811 ■ (*Wilt on High* by Tom Sharpe)?

(b) Have these ISBNs been written down correctly?
- 0 333 38279 X (*This Real Night* by Rebecca West).
- 0 418 53130 9 (*The Growing Pains of Adrian Mole* by Sue Townsend).
- 0 85985 048 X (*Mr Bounce* by Roger Hargreaves).

(c) The ISBN check is not foolproof. Can you find an example where it will break down?

Obviously it would be very tedious for a librarian or bookshop assistant to check ISBN codes by hand, or even using a calculator. But computers are easily programmed to do the check automatically while in the process of handling book orders.

Check digits are used in a wide variety of other instances in which long strings of numbers have to be recorded. They are not always calculated in the same way as the ISBN. The last digit of a reference number is often a check.

IMPORTANT

Read this information page
A Place value

20 From the cradle to the grave

AIM

To develop your skills in
- reading from and plotting graphs
- making step-by-step calculations
- comparing and assessing given data

Introduction

People who work in the medical profession rely on many measurements and calculations. Here are examples from the work of health visitors and nurses.

Health visitors

An important role of the health visitor is to check the growth and development of young children in the community. One thing a health visitor does is measure the height and weight of children at regular intervals: at birth, after 6 weeks, 9 months, 2 years and 3½ years, commonly. In order to compare a particular child's development with the standard in our society, a health visitor might use graphs rather like those shown in Figure 1. Separate graphs are used for boys and girls, but as they are very similar, only one of each (height and weight) has been included here.

Until the age of two, a baby is measured lying flat. This measurement is called the 'supine length'. From age 2 onwards the height when standing is measured. These measurements are recorded to the nearest 0.1 cm. The weight of the child is recorded to the nearest 0.1 kg.

The x-scale (horizontal axis) on both graphs is the age of the child, and it is nowadays recorded as a *decimal* age – the year is divided into 10, not 12!

Examples

A child aged 3 years 6 months is 3.5 years old.
A nine-month-old baby is $\frac{9}{12}$ years old = 0.75 years old.
A six-week-old baby is 0.115 years old:

$$
\begin{aligned}
6 \text{ weeks} &= 42 \text{ days} \\
&= \frac{42}{365} \text{ of a year} \\
&= 0.1150685 \text{ (using a calculator)} \\
&= 0.115 \text{ years (to 3 decimal places)}
\end{aligned}
$$

Task 1

Calculate these ages as decimal fractions of years:
(a) 5 weeks
(b) 7 months
(c) 1 year 4 months

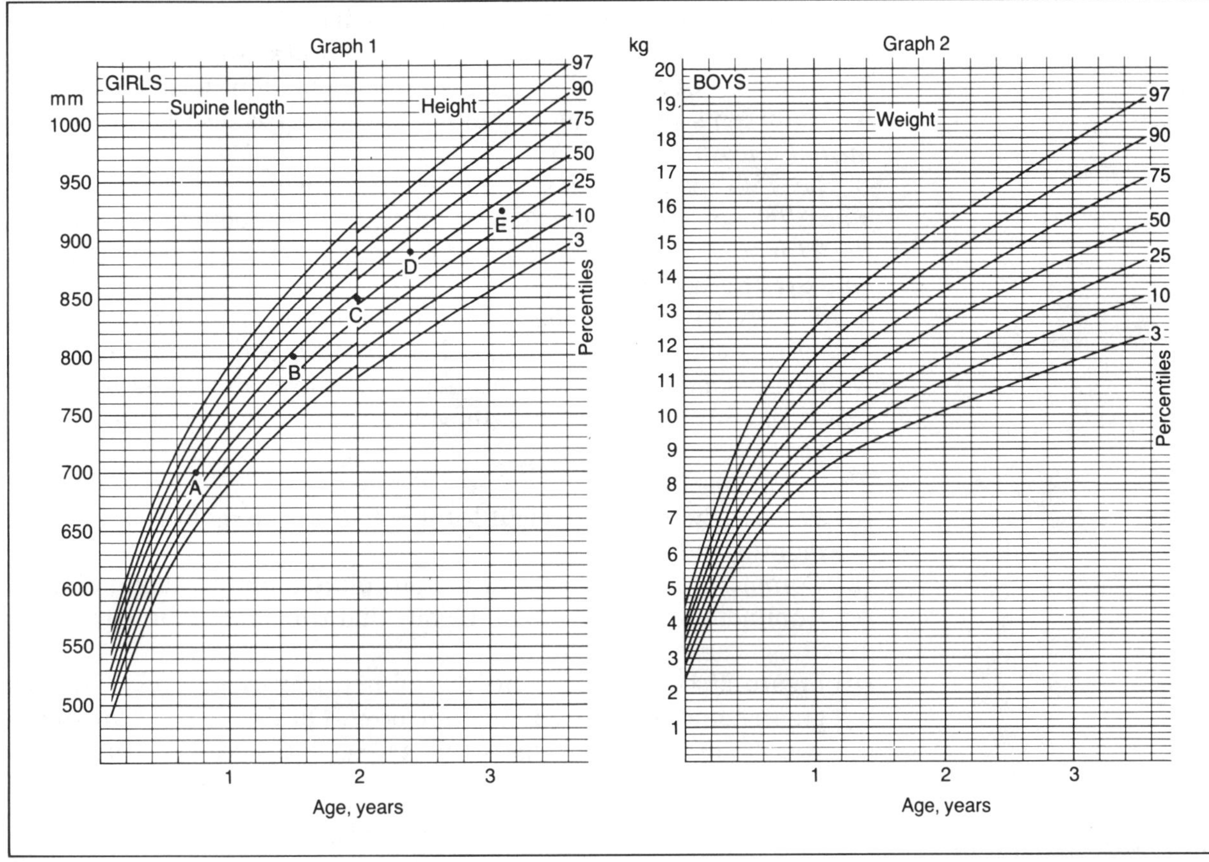

Figure 1 Grids used by health visitors to plot the growth of young children – points A–E are an example (the lines are explained on page 94)

Age and height can now be plotted on the first graph. Age and weight are plotted on the second.

Example

The point A on the height graph for girls is the mark that would be made for a baby aged 0.75 years (9 months), whose height is 700 mm.

Task 2

(a) State the age and height indicated by the marks B, C, D and E on Graph 1.

(b) Copy Graph 2. Plot on it the growth in weight made by the following boy baby:

Decimal age (yr.)	Weight (kg)
0.1	4.0
0.4	6.0
0.9	8.5
1.6	10.5
2.2	11.8
3.05	13.6

The lines drawn on the graphs have been made from statistical surveys of young children. The central line is known as the *50th percentile*, because 50% of all children (50% of the population) would have their measurements plotted on or below this line. It is also known as the *median measurement.*

The 75th percentile line indicates the heights and weights *below* which 75% of children would be. Only 3% of the population are above the 97th percentile. Babies below the 3rd percentile are among the 3% who are the smallest of that age.

As a rough guide, a health visitor would keep a careful eye on youngsters above the 90th and below the 10th percentiles. He or she would be concerned about the health of those above the 97th and below the 3rd percentile until they were proved fit and well.

Task 3

(a) What is the median weight for a boy at ages 6 months, 1 year, 16 months and 2 years?

(b) Comment on the growth of the girl plotted on the height graph.

(c) Comment on the growth of the boy that you plotted for (b) of Task 2.

(d) Figure 2 shows the heights of children at various ages. Plot two graphs, one for girls and one for boys. On the x-axis (horizontal) you should have the age in years; on the y-axis (vertical), the height in millimetres.

Figure 2 Heights of children

Age	Boys			Girls		
	Percentiles			Percentiles		
	5th	50th	95th	5th	50th	95th
3	879	942	1005	876	930	984
6	1068	1143	1218	1059	1138	1217
9	1215	1311	1407	1204	1300	1396
12	1345	1458	1571	1355	1468	1581
15	1504	1633	1762	1507	1603	1699
18	1651	1755	1859	1534	1626	1718

Nurses

A hospital nurse's work involves, as everyone knows, quite a lot of measuring and recording. Body temperature and blood pressure are just two examples.

Another nursing task is to calculate the flow rate for an intravenous infusion, or drip. The flow rate is the number of drops per minute to be fed into the patient's bloodstream, to add to the body the correct volume of fluid over a given length of time. The fluid could be blood, as in a blood transfusion, or a solution of various substances dissolved in water.

The number of drops in one millilitre is as follows:

1 ml blood = 15 drops
1 ml solution = 20 drops

A device for calculating the flow-rate for an intravenous drip

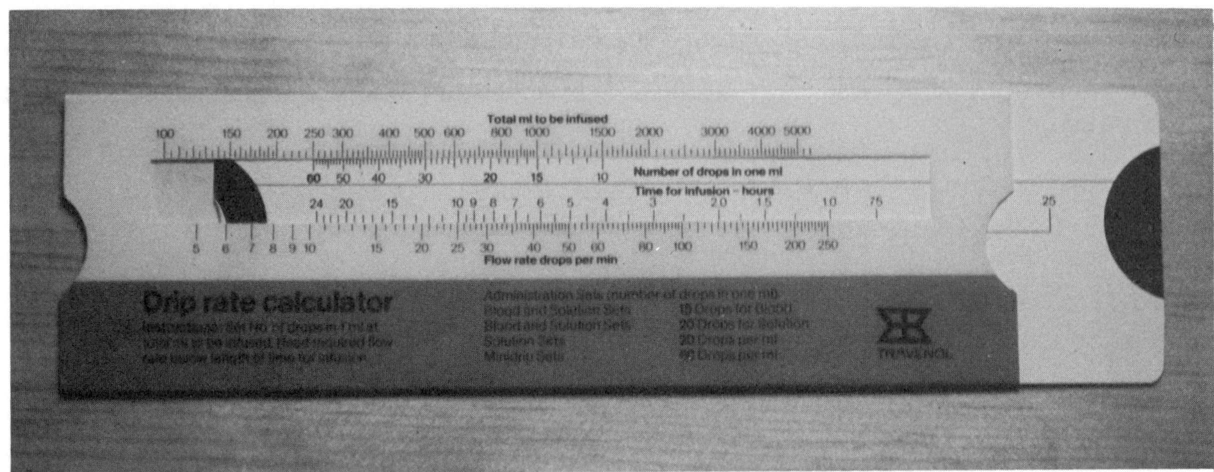

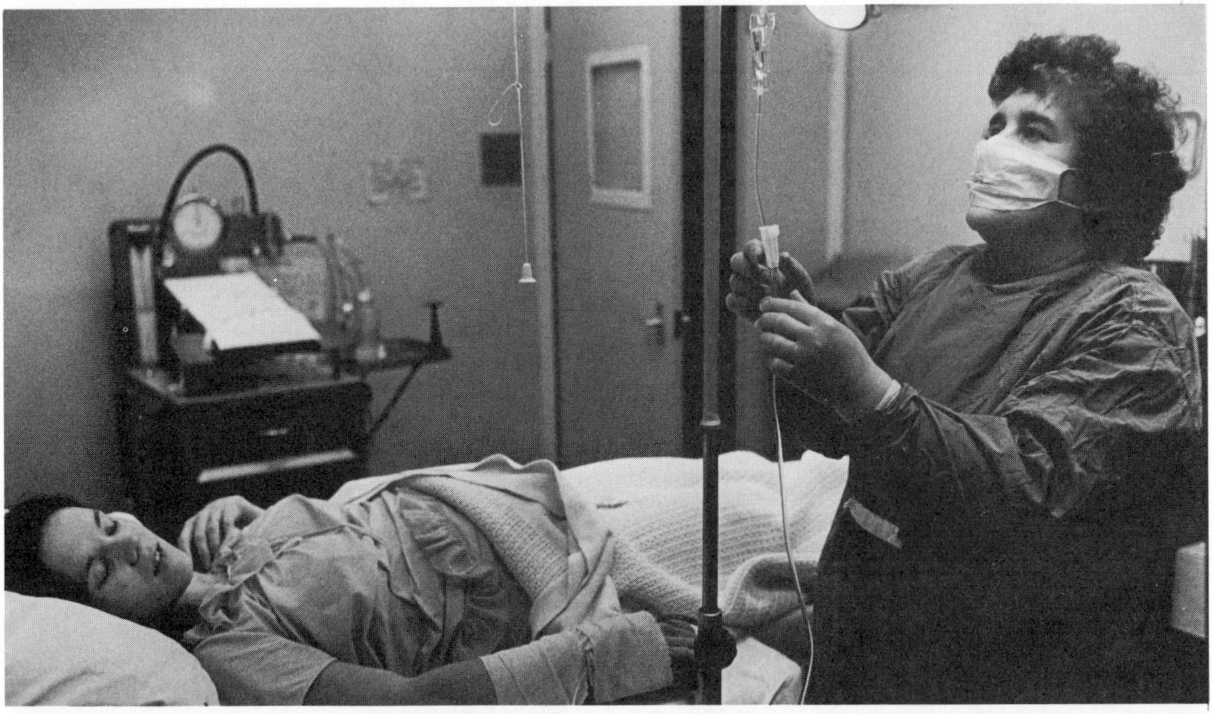

Example
Suppose that in a blood transfusion 1 litre is to go in over eight hours. The problem is to calculate how many drops per minute the equipment should deliver. There are 15 drops in 1 ml of blood

so there are 15000 drops in 1 litre (as 1 l = 1000 ml)
15000 drops in 8 hours
= 1875 drops in 1 hour (15000 ÷ 8)
= 31 drops in 1 minute (1875 ÷ 60 = 31.25; the answer is given to the nearest whole number)

So the equipment must be set at 31 drops per minute.

IMPORTANT

Read these information pages
C Fractions
E Area and volume
F Approximations
G Charts and graphs

Task 4
Calculate the flow rate (the number of drops per minute) for the following intravenous drips.
(a) Solution: 1 litre over 8 hours.
(b) Blood: ½ litre over 5 hours.
(c) Blood: 2 litres over 12 hours.
(d) Solution: ½ litre over 2 hours.
(e) Blood: 3 litres over 20 hours.

Information pages

Place value

To read a number in the decimal system you look at two things:
- the size of the figures; and
- what position each figure is in.

Young children often write their numbers with column headings (H,T,U, etc.) and headings sometimes appear on bank cheques. But usually these headings are missed off.

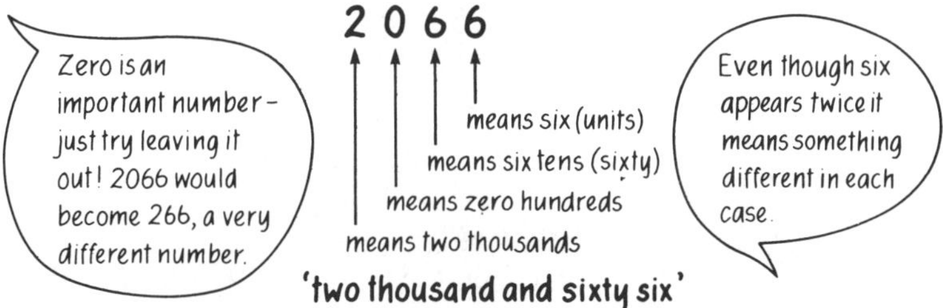

When you use numbers less than one, you need a decimal point. This shows that you are using decimal fractions. Here again, column headings are generally missed off, but the point shows where the (decimal) fraction columns begin.

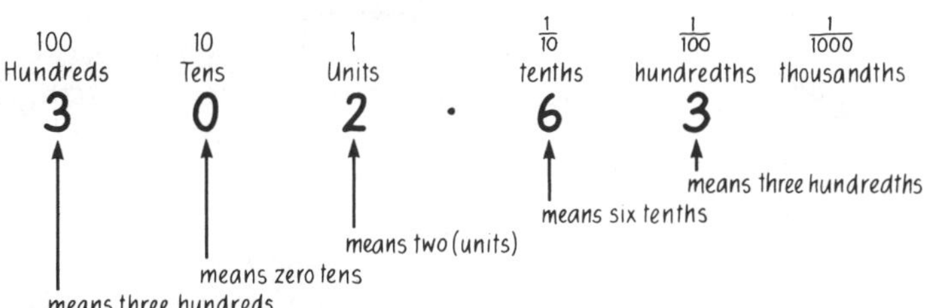

'three hundred and two point six three'

Which number is bigger?

0.4 or 0.39?
0.4 is bigger because it is 4 tenths. 0.39 has only 3 tenths (the extra 9 hundredths aren't as big as a tenth).

6.327 or 6.33?
6.33 is bigger because 3 hundredths is bigger than 2 hundredths plus 7 thousandths. (Both numbers have 6 units and 3 tenths as well.)

B Decimals

Addition

When adding decimal numbers it is important to write them in columns with the decimal points lined up underneath each other.

Example

207.3 + 93 + 0.643 + 6.8 →

```
 207.3
  93.
   0.643
   6.8   +
--------
 307.743
```

Practice

(a) 5.83 + 1.38 (b) 4.2 + 18.8 (c) 5.82 +3.9 (d) 2.6 + 0.632
(e) 56.4 + 11.7 (f) 0.83 + 0.083 (g) 0.8 + 3.7 + 0.53
(h) 9 + 4.6 + 0.8 (i) 16 + 0.52 + 4.6
(j) 23.7 + 0.0082 + 0.924 + 61

Subtraction

Again, put the numbers in columns, lining up the decimal points. Sometimes in order to carry out the subtraction you need to put zeros in 'empty' columns.

Example

```
42.3 - 8.63 → 42.3      → 42.30
               8.63 -      8.63 -
              -----       -----
                          33.67
```

Practice

(a) 17.3 − 9.8 (b) 19.3 − 5.8 (c) 297.8 − 98.9 (d) 5.3 − 0.89
(e) 6 − 0.78 (f) 326.1 − 57.8 (g) 300 − 8.8 (h) 402.2 − 85.4
(i) 400.2 − 7.31 (k) 15.8 − 0.052

Multiplication

When you multiply a decimal number by a whole number, the point does not move.

Example

$5.35 \times 7 \rightarrow$

```
 5.35
  × 7
37.45
```

Practice

(a) 4.26×4 (b) 28.3×6 (c) 22.4×5 (d) 12.57×6 (e) 5.877×9
(f) 0.641×7 (g) 26.22×5 (h) 4.17×7 (i) 0.0082×8
(j) 206.4×4

Division

The point stays in the same place when you divide by a whole number.

Example

$42.12 \div 9 \rightarrow 9\overline{)42.12}$ = 4.68

Practice

(a) $0.8316 \div 9$ (b) $20.4 \div 3$ (c) $0.524 \div 4$ (d) $6.21 \div 9$
(e) $227.2 \div 9$ (f) $4.115 \div 5$ (g) $7.02 \div 4$ (h) $9.5 \div 4$ (i) $11.1 \div 8$
(j) $0.6 \div 8$

Multiplication of two decimal fractions

Carry this out as for ordinary long multiplication, ignoring the decimal point. Put the point in afterwards.

Example

$41.5 \times 3.7 \rightarrow$ (↑ two ↑ places of decimals)

```
  415      [Rough answer: 40 × 3 = 120]
 × 37
 2905
12450
15355 → Answer: 153.55
                    ↑
                    two places of decimals
```

Practice

(a) 36.2×3.1 (b) 4.2×40.6 (c) 39.5×3.9 (d) 51.4×0.83
(e) 6.22×0.34 (f) 22.8×0.6 (g) 3.38×2.4 (h) 0.418×5.3
(i) 0.339×0.52 (j) 41.73×0.57

C Fractions

A fraction is part of a whole. Now we are changing to the metric system of measurement in the UK, ordinary fractions (which look like this: $\frac{1}{2}$, $\frac{7}{8}$) are being replaced by decimal fractions (which look like this: 0.5, 0.875). But whichever way they are written, we still need to understand them.

Equivalent fractions

The same-sized number can be written as different fractions.

Examples

$\frac{1}{2} = \frac{2}{4} = \frac{4}{8} = \frac{8}{16}$ and so on.

$\frac{1}{5} = \frac{2}{10} = \frac{3}{15} = \frac{4}{20}$ and so on. $\frac{1}{5} = \frac{1 \times 7}{5 \times 7} = \frac{7}{35}$.

$\frac{6}{8}$ is the same as $\frac{3}{4}$ because $\frac{6 \div 2}{8 \div 2} = \frac{3}{4}$. $\frac{3}{4}$ cannot be simplified.

Practice
Simplify these fractions:

(a) $\frac{5}{25}$ (b) $\frac{16}{32}$ (c) $\frac{12}{16}$ (d) $\frac{8}{10}$ (e) $\frac{45}{100}$

Mixed numbers

Top-heavy fractions, like $\frac{9}{4}$, can be changed into a whole number and a fractional part.

Example

$\frac{9}{4} = \frac{8}{4} + \frac{1}{4} = 2 + \frac{1}{4} = 2\frac{1}{4}$

$2\frac{1}{4}$ is called a mixed number.

Practice
Change these top-heavy fractions to mixed numbers:

(a) $\frac{10}{8}$ (b) $\frac{15}{4}$ (c) $\frac{10}{4}$ (d) $\frac{43}{10}$ (e) $\frac{7}{2}$

Changing to decimal fractions

Fractions can be changed to decimal fractions.

Example

$\frac{3}{8}$ means $3 \div 8 = 0.375$ (using a calculator)

Practice
Change these fractions to decimal fractions:

(a) $\frac{7}{8}$ (b) $\frac{4}{5}$ (c) $\frac{7}{10}$ (d) $\frac{53}{100}$ (e) $\frac{2}{7}$

Changing to percentages

Fractions can be changed to percentages: 1 whole = 100%.

Example

$\frac{3}{8}$ is $\frac{3}{8}$ of $100\% = \frac{3}{8} \times 100\% = \frac{300}{8}\% = 37.5\%$

Practice
Change these fractions to percentages:

(a) $\frac{3}{5}$ (b) $\frac{3}{4}$ (c) $\frac{1}{10}$ (d) $\frac{3}{16}$ (e) $\frac{1}{3}$

Adding and subtracting

Fractions can be added and subtracted, but only when they have been changed so that they have the same bottom number. This changing is done using equivalent fractions.

Examples

$$\frac{7}{10} - \frac{3}{10} = \frac{4}{10}$$

$$\frac{1}{4} + \frac{1}{8} = \frac{2}{8} + \frac{1}{8} = \frac{3}{8}$$

$$\frac{9}{10} - \frac{1}{4} = \frac{18}{20} - \frac{5}{20} = \frac{13}{20}$$

$$\left(\frac{9 \times 2}{10 \times 2} = \frac{18}{20} \text{ and } \frac{1 \times 5}{4 \times 5} = \frac{5}{20}\right)$$

Practice

(a) $\frac{1}{4} + \frac{1}{2}$ (b) $\frac{5}{8} - \frac{1}{4}$ (c) $\frac{11}{16} - \frac{1}{2}$

(d) $\frac{7}{10} + \frac{1}{4}$ (e) $\frac{4}{10} + \frac{29}{100}$

Multiplying by whole numbers

Examples

$$3 \times \frac{1}{4} = \frac{3}{4}$$

$$4 \times 2\frac{1}{5} = 8 + \frac{4}{5} = 8\frac{4}{5}$$

$$6 \times 1\frac{1}{4} = 6 + \frac{6}{4} = 6 + 1\frac{2}{4} = 7\frac{2}{4} = 7\frac{1}{2}$$

Practice

(a) $5 \times 2\frac{1}{4}$ (b) $3 \times 1\frac{7}{10}$ (c) $8 \times 2\frac{1}{5}$ (d) $6 \times 1\frac{3}{10}$ (e) $8 \times 3\frac{1}{4}$

In fact you can multiply fractions by fractions, and divide fractions by fractions.

Changing decimal fractions to fractions

To do this it is best to think of the column headings that belong above the decimal fraction.

Examples

tenths hundredths
↓ ↓
0. 5 3 so $0.53 = \frac{53}{100}$

tenths hundredths thousandths
↓ ↓ ↓
0. 1 2 1 so $0.121 = \frac{121}{1000}$

Sometimes the fraction can be simplified.

Example

tenths hundredths

$$0.\underset{\downarrow}{4}\,\underset{\downarrow}{8} = \frac{48}{100} \text{ and } \frac{48 \div 4}{100 \div 4} = \frac{12}{25} \text{ so } 0.48 = \frac{12}{25}$$

Practice

Change these decimal fractions to fractions:
(a) 0.9 (b) 0.421 (c) 0.72 (d) 0.555 (e) 2.8

Percentages

1% MEANS $\frac{1}{100}$

ONE PERCENT

ONE PER HUNDRED

1% of something is a *hundredth* of it.
So 1% of £400, say, is $\frac{1}{100} \times$ £400 or £400 $\div$ 100 = £4.

$25\% = \frac{25}{100}$ and $\frac{25}{100} \overset{\div 25}{=} \frac{1}{4}$ so $25\% = \frac{1}{4}$ (a *quarter*).

So 25% of £400 is $\frac{1}{4} \times$ £400 or £400 $\div$ 4 = £100.

$10\% = \frac{10}{100}$ and $\frac{10}{100} \overset{\div 10}{=} \frac{1}{10}$ so $10\% = \frac{1}{10}$ (a *tenth*).

$50\% = \frac{50}{100}$ and $\frac{50}{100} \overset{\div 50}{=} \frac{1}{2}$ so $50\% = \frac{1}{2}$ (a *half*).

$33\frac{1}{3}\% = \frac{33\frac{1}{3}}{100}$ and $\frac{33\frac{1}{3}}{100} \overset{\div 33\frac{1}{3}}{=} \frac{1}{3}$ so $33\frac{1}{3}\% = \frac{1}{3}$ (a *third*).

Example
A *discount* of 33⅓% means ⅓ (a third) off. So a discount of 33⅓% on £450 is a discount of ⅓ × £450 or £450 ÷ 3 = £150.
The discounted price is then £450 − £150 = £300.

Practice
(a) What are the following percentages as fractions:
• 30% • 5% • 20% • 75%?
(b) What is 25% of £600?
(c) What is 20% of £5.25 (525p)?
(d) What is 15% of £2.20? (Work out 10% first, then 5% and add the results together.)
(e) What is the new price after a 10% discount on the following:
• £9.00 • £12.50 • £5.99?

FINDING 1%
OF AN AMOUNT
OF MONEY IS EASY
1% of £34 = 34p
1% of £16.32 = 16.32p

Another way

To find a percentage of a quantity: first work out 1% of the amount, then multiply by the percentage you want.

Example
Find 8% of £12.50.

1% of £12.50 = 12.50p
so 8% of £12.50 = 8 × 12.5p
= 100p
= £1

Using a calculator

Many calculators have a percentage key: [%]
To find 8% of £12.50 press these keys:
[8] [%] [×] [1] [2] [.] [5] [=]

Area and volume

Area

Area is the amount of flat space that a shape takes up. It is measured in square metres, square millimetres, square feet and so on.

You find the area A of a rectangle by multiplying its length l by its width w.

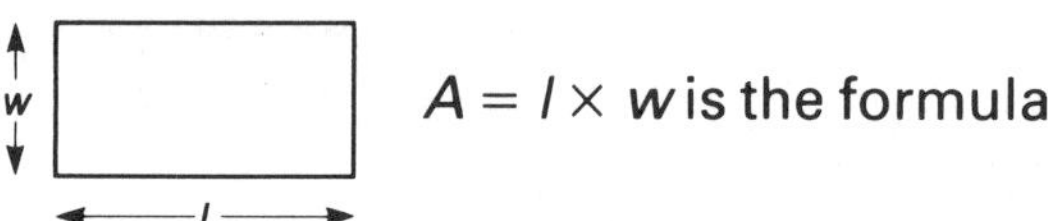

$A = l \times w$ is the formula

You must make sure that these two measurements are in the same units.

Examples

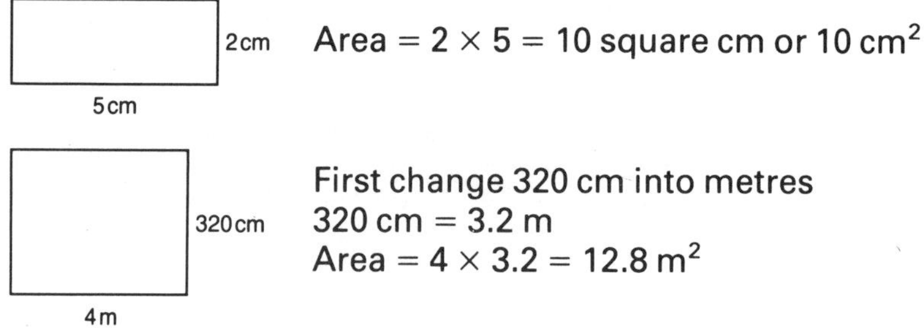

Area $= 2 \times 5 = 10$ square cm or $10\ \text{cm}^2$

First change 320 cm into metres
320 cm = 3.2 m
Area $= 4 \times 3.2 = 12.8\ \text{m}^2$

Practice
Find the areas of these rectangles:
(a) 4 cm × 3 cm (b) 2 ft. × 3½ ft. (c) 3 cm × 25 mm
(d) 2 m × 125 cm (e) 30 mm square

You can find the areas of some more complicated shapes if you can treat them as a combination of rectangles . . .

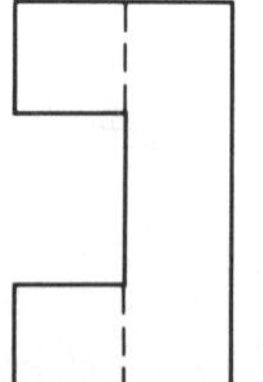

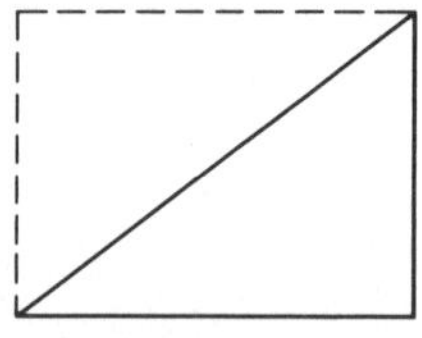

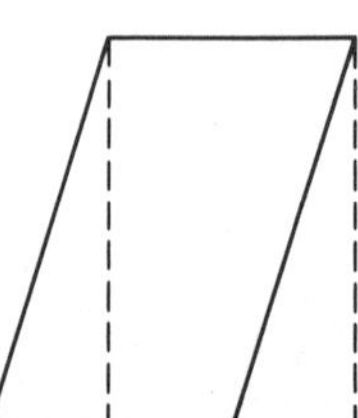

The area of a circle can be found using the formula πr^2.

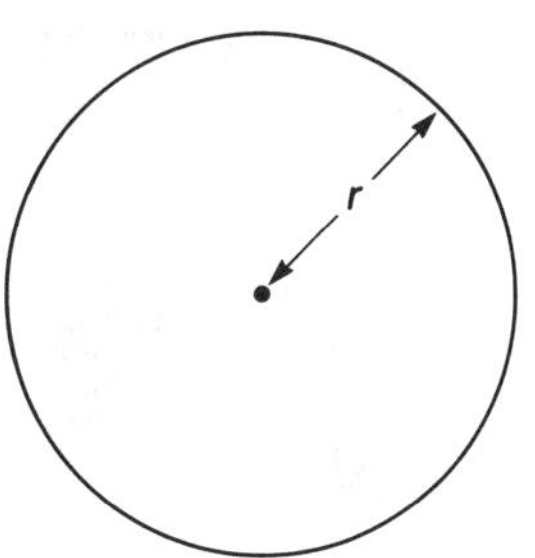

r is the radius
π, called 'pi', is a constant number. It has a value 3.14159 . . . (these figures go on for ever). $\pi = 3$ is a reasonable approximation.

Example
The area of a circle with radius 4 cm is $\pi \times 4 \times 4 = 3 \times 4 \times 4 = 48$ cm^2 (approximately).

Volume

You find the volume of a rectangular box by multiplying its length l by its width w by its height h.

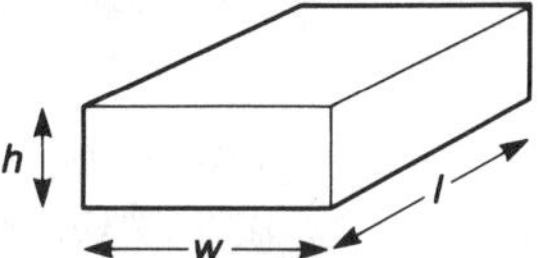

$V = l \times w \times h$ is the formula

(Remember always to work with the same units of measurement.)

Example

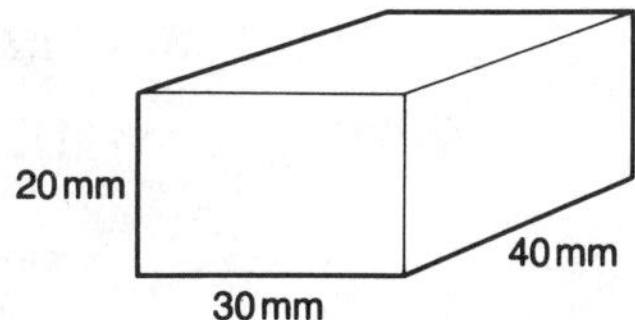

$$\begin{aligned} \text{Volume} &= 40 \times 30 \times 20 \\ &= 1200 \times 20 \\ &= 24\,000 \text{ mm}^3 \end{aligned}$$

Practice
Find the volume of these boxes:
(a) 2 cm × 5 cm × 2 cm (b) 3 cm × 4 cm × 25 cm
(c) 1 ft. × 1¼ ft. × 2 ft.

F Approximations

There are two important ways of approximating numbers that you should know about:

- significant figures; and
- decimal places.

Significant figures

Example

Consider 92.6762. This number has six figures. You get an approximation if you use only *three* figures, like this:

92·6⑦62

You are interested in the biggest three figures (92.6) *but* the next figure is a seven, which is over half way – so you round up to:

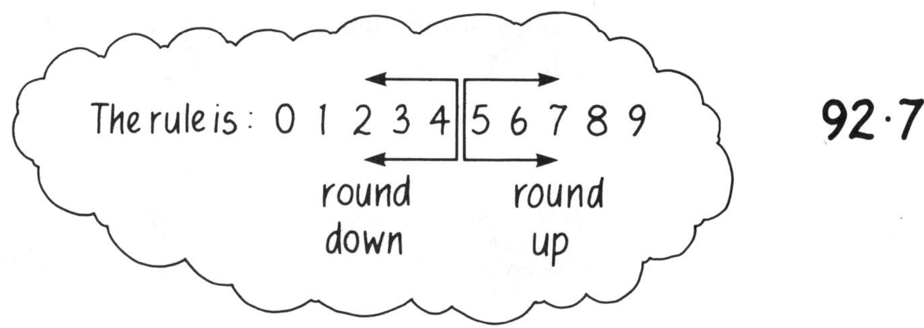

92·7

More examples

8 .②01 is 8 to 1 significant figure (1 sig. fig.)

0 . 245⑤1 is 0.246 to 3 sig. fig.

0 . 0072⑥is 0.0073 to 2 sig. fig.

10②. 6 is 100 to 2 sig. fig.

99 .⑥3 is 100 to 2 sig. fig.

Practice
Round these numbers as given:
(a) 7.28 to 2 sig. fig. (b) 19.07 to 3 sig. fig. (c) 2362 to 2 sig. fig.
(d) 0.014 to 1 sig. fig. (e) 0.00235 to 2 sig. fig
(f) 83.646 to 4 sig. fig (g) 0.0982 to 1 sig. fig. (h) 174 to 2 sig. fig.
(i) 89.2473 to 4 sig. fig. (j) 998.7 to 2 sig. fig.

Decimal places

This way of approximating only looks at the decimal fractions – the figures to the right of the decimal point.

Example
Consider 92.6762 again. This number has four decimal places.
Rounding to three decimal places is done like this:

92·676(2)

these are the decimal places you are interested in

the next figure is a two – you round down (using the same rule) to: **92·676**

More examples

8 . 20①is 8.20 to 2 decimal places.

0 . 24⑤51 is 0.25 to 2 decimal places.

32 . 2④52 is 32.2 to 1 decimal place.

0 . 0245⑤1 is 0.0246 to 4 decimal places.

Practice
Round these numbers as given:
(a) 8.36 to 1 decimal place (b) 63.251 to 2 decimal places
(c) 0.725 to 2 decimal places (d) 0.0883 to 2 decimal places
(e) 7.4318 to 3 decimal places (f) 0.0883 to 2 sig. fig.
(g) 63.251 to 1 sig. fig. (h) 7.825 to 2 decimal places
(i) 7.285 to 2 sig. fig. (j) 7.4396 to 3 decimal places

Why?

All measurements are approximate. However precise you try to make a measurement, there will always be better equipment that would make a more accurate one.

When measuring you should always think about the *level of accuracy* needed. If you are measuring a room to buy paint and wallpaper, you don't have to work in millimetres – centimetres will do. A glazier would have to work in millimetres though, otherwise a pane of glass might fall straight through the frame! An atomic scientist measures lengths much tinier than millimetres.

When you do calculations with measurements, say to find the area of a floor covering, your result might be a long string of figures suggesting great accuracy. This is misleading: the result cannot be more accurate than the approximate measurements that you started with. So you must round the answer to at least the same degree of approximation that you used for your original measurements.

Example

You measure your kitchen floor so that you can estimate the cost of a new floor covering. The floor is 3.24 m by 4.10 m.

Area $= 3.24\text{ m} \times 4.10\text{ m} = 13.284\text{ m}^2$ (using a calculator)

As the measurements were taken to 3 significant figures, the *area* should be rounded to 3 significant figures as well.

Area $= 3.24\text{ m} \times 4.10\text{ m} = 13.3\text{ m}^2$ (to 3 sig. fig.)

Charts and graphs

Co-ordinates

A co-ordinate is a pair of numbers which gives a point on a grid. The *x*-value is given first, followed by the *y*-value.

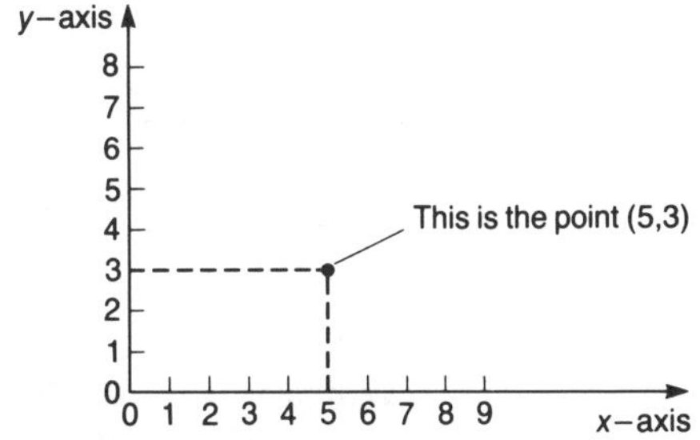

Axes

Generally there should be equal spaces on an axis between values corresponding to equal increases. The *x*-axis and the *y*-axis can be different.

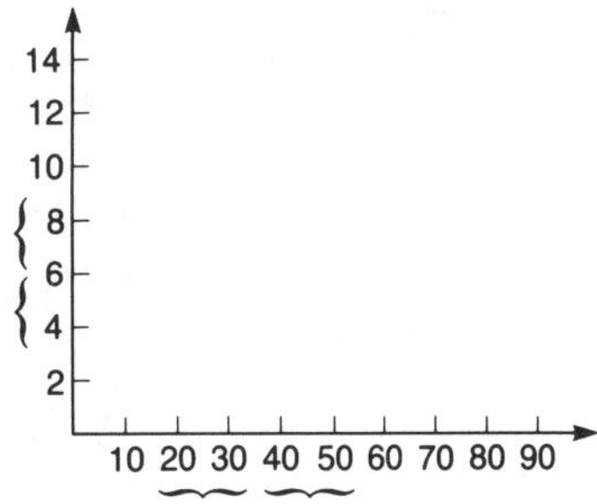

Line graph

A line graph can be made by joining co-ordinate pairs in order.

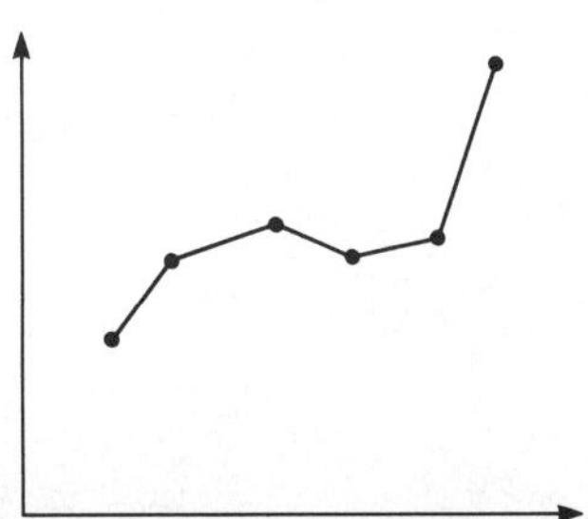

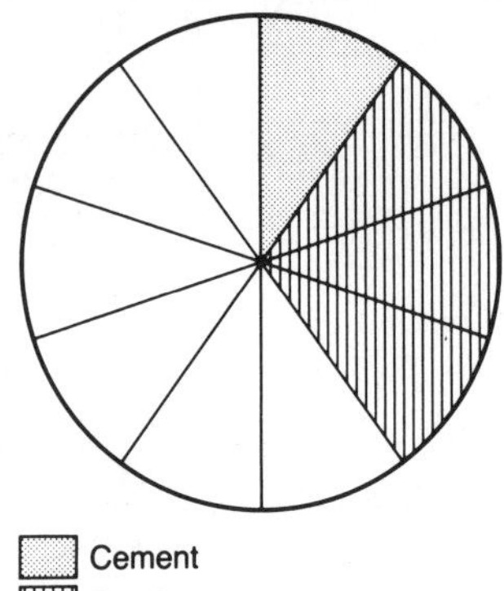

Pie charts

Pie charts show how something is split into separate parts.

Example
Concrete can b made with 1 part cement to 3 parts sand to 6 parts aggregate = 10 parts altogether.

Drawing pie charts
To make a pie chart you need a protractor. First, work out how many parts you have altogether. Then 360° ÷ number of parts gives you the angle in degrees for each part.

Pie charts from percentages
Sometimes you draw pie charts starting from percentages. This means that the pie chart must be split into 100 parts (because 100% = 1 whole). Each part will be 360° ÷ 100 = 3.6°. So 1% is represented by 3.6° on the pie chart.
44% will be represented by:

$$44 \times 3.6 = 158.4° \text{ (0.4° is very hard to draw)}$$
$$= 158° \text{ (to the nearest degree)}$$

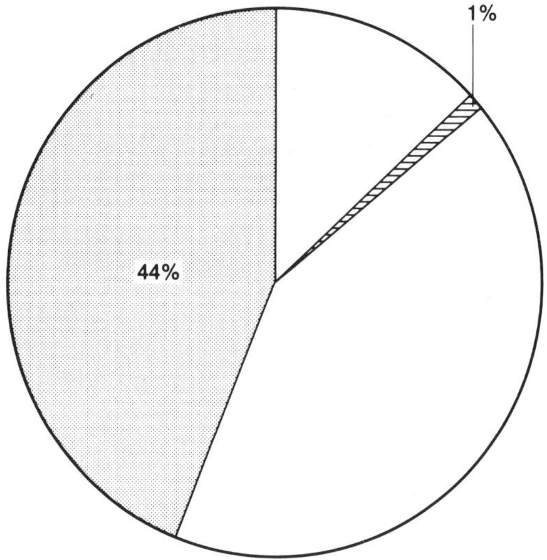

Averages

Averages are rather like Members of Parliament (MPs). Both are representatives.

An MP is supposed to represent the people in an area (the constituency). An average represents a collection of pieces of information.

Sometimes an MP is a good representative. Other MPs are not so good. It is the same with averages.

There are three types of average which are commonly used:

- mode;
- median; and
- mean.

The mode

This is the most often occurring or the most popular quantity or quality.

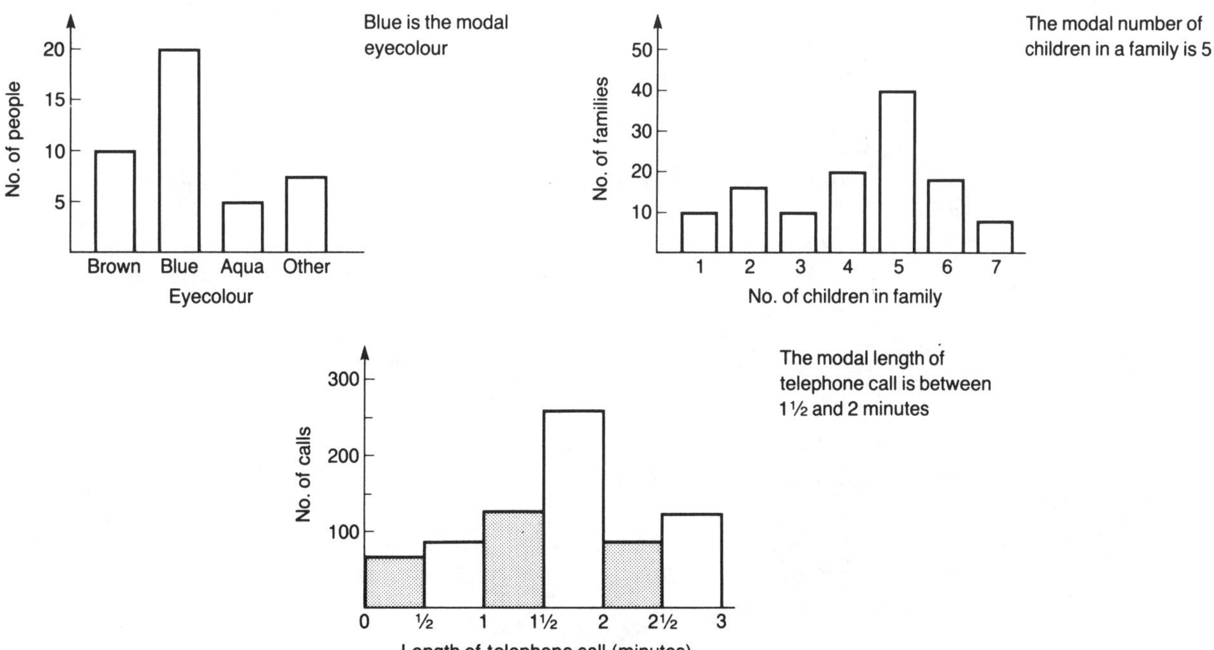

An MP in Britain is most like the mode. This is because he or she has received the greatest number of votes from the electors.

The median

This can only be given for numerical data, such as measurements or counts. You find it by listing the numbers in order, from smallest to largest. Then you pick out the middle number.

Example
The median of {7, 6, 6, 2, 3} → 2, 3, 6, 6, 7 → the median is 6.
The median of {4, 2, 10, 5, 13, 12} → 2, 4, 5, 10, 12, 13 → the median is 7½ (the mid-point of 5 and 10).

The mean

You find the mean by adding up the individual pieces of data (which again can only be numbers); then you divide by the number of pieces of data.

Example
The mean of {7, 6, 6, 2, 3} → 7 + 6 + 6 + 2 + 3 = 24 → 24 ÷ 5 = 4.8 → the mean is 4.8.

The range

It is often useful to note the spread of a set of figures. To calculate this you simply take away the smallest number from the largest. The result is called the *range* of the figures.

Example
The range of {7, 6, 6, 2, 3} → 7 − 2 = 5 → the range is 5.

Practice
Work out the mode, median, mean and range of these sets of information:
(a) {1, 12, 2, 2, 4}
(b) {2, 5, 6, 5, 5, 2, 6, 1, 1, 7}
(c) {4, 8, 3}
(d) {6, 10, 12, 6, 2, 2}
(e) {4, 9, 2, 2, 1, 7, 8, 10}

Twenty-four-hour clock

You'll find the 24-hour clock on timetables, some digital clocks and in many other places. You recognise it when the time is written as 4 figures, e.g. 14.25. Often you need to be able to convert between the 12-hour clock and the 24-hour clock – for instance, when you set a video recorder to record a TV programme. You use 24-hour clock times on the video but the *Radio Times* or *TV Times* or newspaper tells you the programme times using the 12-hour clock.

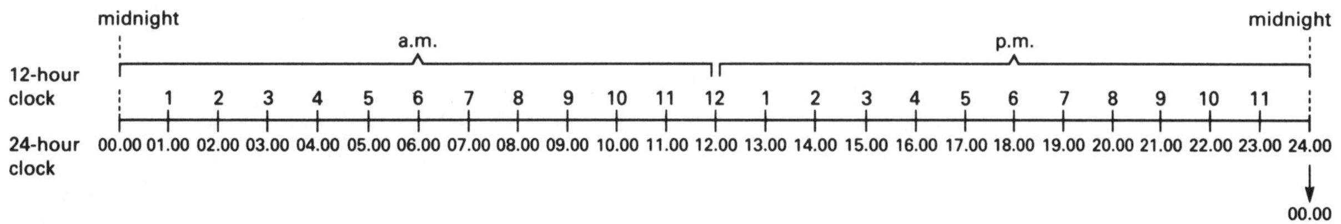

This is simple for times before midday.

Examples

2 a.m. = 02.00
3.30 a.m. = 03.30
10.45 a.m. = 10.45

At midday the 24-hour clock carries on counting the hours – 13, 14, 15, . . .

Examples

3.00 p.m. = 15.00
4.30 p.m. = 16.30
8.40 p.m. = 20.40

Practice

(a) Convert these times to the 24-hour clock:
- 5.30 a.m. • 7.30 p.m. • 3.45 p.m. • 11.36 a.m.
- 11.36 p.m.

(b) Convert these times to the 12-hour clock. Remember to say whether the result is a.m. or p.m.
- 12.00 • 02.50 • 11.37 • 18.25 • 20.42

J Calculator

Buying a calculator

Before you go out to buy a calculator, think about these points.

Will you want to carry it around with you?
Thin, light ones will fit in your pocket but larger calculators are easier to use because the keys will be better spaced.

What do you need to use it for?
For most people a basic calculator will do. It will add, subtract, multiply and divide. It will have a percentage key, a memory and maybe a square-root key.

Some calculators are specialised in certain tasks; for example they may do metric conversions automatically. Do you need something like this?

Others may have clocks, alarms, calendars, musical chimes, etc. Don't be too impressed with these gimmicks. Usually you can tell the time by looking at your watch.

Lots of calculators will turn themselves off after ten minutes or so if you forget. This is quite a useful feature, especially if you are absent-minded!

Scientific calculators will work out logarithms, cosines, standard deviations, etc. Will any of these functions be necessary for you?

What is the best kind to buy?
Make sure you buy a calculator with a liquid-crystal display (LCD) as these need very little battery power to run them. LCDs are dark-grey figures on a light-grey background. Silver-oxide batteries last longer than alkaline ones. They are more expensive but they will give more than 500 hours of continuous use. Some calculators need no batteries as they get power from solar cells.

How easy is it to use?
Test how easy the keyboard is to use. Is it carefully laid out? Check that you understand how to use the memory. Does the calculator have a clear instruction book?

If you cannot decide, talk to your teacher about it or read the latest calculator report in *Which?* magazine. You should find it in the library.

Using your calculator

Use the instruction book to help you learn to use your calculator fully. Practise the key sequences needed to carry out different operations. Practise using the calculator's memory.

Whenever possible, work out the rough answer to your calculation before you do it on the calculator. It is very easy to make a mistake when keying in the numbers and so you could get a completely wrong answer. A rough answer would help you spot this.

Don't become dependent on the calculator. You mustn't lose the ability to make calculations in your head. You won't always have a calculator with you, and even if you did it might be embarrassing to use it (for instance, to check your change in a shop).

This book is to be returned on or before
the last date stamped below.

12 MAY 1998

-7 DEC 1999

- 2 NOV 2005

LIBREX

MUSGROVE

104005

LIVERPOOL INSTITUTE OF
HIGHER EDUCATION
THE MARKLAND LIBRARY